AT A GLANCE

The Church Year Teaching Schedule

ADVENT and CHRISTMAS: THEME—"SIGNS OF THE KINGDOM"

Groups can start at the beginning of any season in the year.

- ❑ **ADVENT** (6 weeks)—in December
- ❑ **EPIPHANY / ORDINARY TIME** (10 weeks)—in January
- ❑ **LENT** (6 weeks)—leading up to Easter
- ❑ **EASTER** (7 weeks)—from Easter to Pentecost
- ❑ **FALL** (12 weeks)—the last 12 weeks of Pentecost / Ordinary Time

EPIPHANY / ORDINARY TIME*: THEME—"THE LIGHT OF THE WORLD"

LENT: THEME—"STANDING UP TO THE TEST"

* In the Roman Catholic tradition, Epiphany and Pentecost are referred to as Ordinary Time.

SEARCH THE SCRIPTURE

PASTOR'S GUIDEBOOK
YEAR A

SERENDIPITY EXECUTIVE EDITOR:
Lyman Coleman

AUTHOR:
Keith Madsen

LAYOUT PRODUCTION TEAM:
Sharon Penington
Erika Tiepel
Christopher Werner
Andrew Sloan
Cathy Tardif

Serendipity House • P.O. Box 1012 • Littleton, CO 80160
TOLL FREE 1-800-525-9563 / www.serendipityhouse.com

MAP

Table of Contents

A Word to the Pastor

You are the key to this program. You are the cheerleader, the conductor, the head coach, the pacesetter and the vision-caster. Your job is crucial, but not impossible.

If you really want your people in small groups, where they can share their life and care for one another, you can make it happen.

You do not need to know everything about cars to drive a car, and you do not need to know everything about small groups to run this program.

Trust us! We have put together a model for healthy, balanced small groups for a church that you can launch and direct from the pulpit without additional energy on your part.

This program is:

- **Low budget**—All you need for the groups is the handout which you can reproduce on the church copier.

- **Low risk**—The teaching from the pulpit will help the groups stay focused.

- **No homework**—The sermon is the preparation for the group study.

- **High involvement**—Anyone who attends church can belong to a group.

- **No babysitting required**—Groups can meet right after the worship service in church while the children are in Sunday school.

- **Healthy balance**—Scripture from the sermon is balanced with personal application and prayer in groups.

- **Very little leadership skills needed**—The handout provides a three-part agenda and a guided questionnaire for discussion.

Your sermon teaching based on the Scripture text is critical to prepare the groups for their own sharing. In fact, we suggest that you refer to the small group handout in your sermon and possibly share your own answer to one or two of the questions.

Here's to the new thing that God is going to do through you and the small group program in your church.

Here's to the beautiful people in your church who are going to experience something new in their spiritual pilgrimage.

Here's to a great God who has called us into this new adventure.

A Healthy Balance

This program will help you balance two crucial aspects of congregational life—the teaching from the pulpit and the process of your people assimilating that teaching and caring for each other. Any individual or existing group who attends the Sunday morning worship service can be involved in this program: youth, adults, couples, singles, seniors, men's fellowships, women's fellowships, Sunday school classes, the choir, ushers, official board, church staff, ministry teams, as well as small groups.

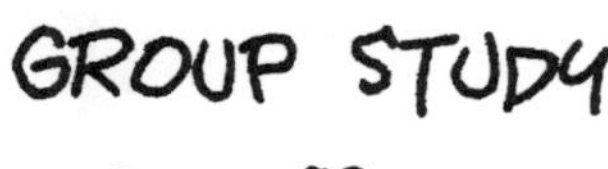

SUNDAY TEACHING: The program is based on the Scripture lesson from the Gospel readings for the church year in the Lectionary, beginning with Advent (around the first of December).

This program can be used for any season of the church year: Advent and Christmas (6 weeks), Epiphany (or Ordinary Time; 10 weeks), Lent (6 weeks), Easter (7 weeks) and the last 12 weeks of Pentecost (or Ordinary Time) in the fall (12 weeks). (There's a break in the curriculum for the summer.)

SMALL GROUPS: Following the Sunday morning worship service, small groups can meet to discuss the Scripture lesson and care for one another. A small group:

- starts with 3 people and can grow up to 12

- meets for 60 to 90 minutes

- follows the 3-part agenda in the handout

- lasts for 6 to 7 weeks and then decides to renew their covenant for another session or to disband

- terminates at the end of the Easter season (around the end of May) and/or makes a new covenant to start again in the fall

- keeps an "empty chair" and seeks to bring new people into the group as part of their mission

SERMONS
ADMINI-
STRATION
COUNSELING
STAFF
VISITATION
COMMITTEES
WORSHIP
SMALL
GROUPS
FINANCES
PANIC!

Before You Push the Panic Button

Again, you are crucial to this program—but your job doesn't have to be overwhelming. Using this *Pastor's Guidebook*, you should be able to accomplish some basic goals that we're sure every pastor would long for—meaningful sermons that people not only remember but discuss with one another, while at the same time, "searching the Scripture" and caring for each other.

As pastor, you have three roles in making this program successful:

1. Vision-caster: You need to spark an interest in your congregation for small groups in general, and in this opportunity for a unified pulpit-based program in particular.

2. Cheerleader: Use your influence to encourage people to serve as leaders, to get into one of the groups, and to invite others to join them.

3. Pacesetter: Your people will not likely share in their groups at a deeper level than you share in your sermon. It is crucial that you model personal sharing pertaining to the group sessions as part of your preaching. This will set your congregation free to "go deeper" themselves.

You will notice that the sessions in this book (beginning on page 29) follow closely the material in the handouts. The Introduction to the session, the Study notes, the Personal Question and the Story are all meant to help you prepare your sermon. The more you incorporate these—and perhaps other questions from the handout—the more prepared and inspired people will be when they gather in their groups.

The Serendipity principles of Bible study help to "level the playing field"—so that everyone, no matter how much church and Scripture background they have or don't have, can equally participate. This program accomplishes this in the following ways.

- starting with an ice-breaker
- moving across the "disclosure scale" from low risk to high risk by sharing "your story" with the Scripture story
- open-ended "right-brain" questions that encourage rather than shut down discussion
- multiple-choice options—which are easier to answer for those who are shy, know little about the Bible, or are new Christians
- tight agenda which helps people who are already uncomfortable feel less threatened
- the "fearless foursome" which breaks down a large group into a size where sharing and discussion happen best

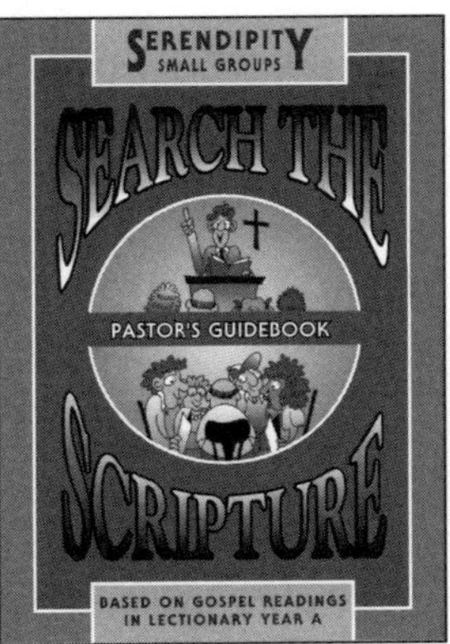

The Small Group Handout

The handout has been carefully designed to lead the group meeting without the group even knowing it.

There are three parts to the agenda which are built into this handout.

GATHERING TIME / 10 minutes: To help the group relax and "unpack" at the beginning of the session, the handout provides an ice-breaker to start the sharing on the easy side and "level the playing field" for anyone who is shy and reticent about sharing.

STORY / SCRIPTURE / 30 minutes: For the Study time, the handout provides two steps. Step One: Story. This is a case study of someone in church history (past or present) who lived out the lesson in the Scripture passage. Step Two: Scripture. The Gospel text that formed the basis for the sermon is repeated so that the group can refer to the passage in their sharing.

The group has the option of skipping the Story in the handout and moving immediately to the Scripture lesson if time is limited.

QUESTIONS: A guided questionnaire is provided for the group. The flow of the questions is carefully designed to lead a group across the "disclosure scale" from easy to heavy sharing. All of the questions are open-ended. There are no right or wrong answers, and many of the questions are followed by multiple-choice options to make the sharing even easier.

STUDY NOTES: Reference helps are provided—definitions of key words, historical background and running commentary. This will enable those who are not familiar with the Bible text to "keep up to speed" in the group.

CARING TIME / 20–40 minutes: The most important time is the last 20–40 minutes in the meeting. The sharing is facilitated by asking the question: "How can we help you in prayer this week?" At the close, the leader can either: (1) close in prayer, (2) ask volunteers to pray for the specific prayer requests; or (3) allow the group to pray spontaneously.

WE'RE ALMOST THERE PASTOR!
PASTOR

How to Lighten the Load

Some churches utilizing this material will use it as part of an already developed small group ministry. If that's the case with your church, you have our permission to skip this section! But for many churches, this may be your first foray into intentional small group ministry. Welcome to the adventure! Just like when you buy a VCR or home computer, it's good to take time to look at the manual to know how to set it up, so you will want to look through this section to see how to "set up" your small group ministry. Of course, we don't have an LCD clock that will blink at you forever if you fail to do so, but it will help your ministry function better if you do! Here is what we suggest:

1. **Get the church board on board.** This program thrives best when the whole church is behind it. Outline the proposed ministry to your board, and make sure all their questions are answered. Make clear to your board members that voting for this ministry means they will participate themselves and encourage others to do so as well!

2. **Appoint a leadership team.** You need leadership who will guide and maintain the overall small group ministry, and leadership for each small group. The nature of the team that will lead the overall ministry will depend on the size of your church. Small churches will need to appoint someone within the Christian Education Committee to have responsibility for this ministry. Medium to large churches (over 200 members) should consider a leadership team set up specifically to guide and maintain this ministry. Who should be on this team? Let's consider Jesus' example. After a night in prayer, Jesus chose 12 individuals to share his vision. Some of them were not all that religious, but they had three qualities. They were faithful, available and teachable. Not one individual possessed all of the gifts, but together they became the body of Christ in the world.

    You should try to have people of passion and vision on your team, such as:

    - the senior pastor (the head cheerleader—vision-caster)
    - an executive-type who knows how to recruit, train and supervise
    - a political activist who thinks big and dreams big
    - someone with enthusiasm who knows how to sell the vision to others
    - a prayer warrior who can call down angels from heaven
    - someone who has experienced some real pain in life

3. **Recruit and train leaders.** Every small group also has a leadership team of three people: the Leader, the Apprentice, and the Host. The Leader will be convening the sessions, modeling honest sharing, and encouraging participation. The Apprentice is one who observes the Leader so that he or she can lead a group in the future. The Host provides the home, provides or coordinates the provision of refreshments and helps make sure group members are comfortable. This person is also important in inviting people they know who are on the fringe of the church to be part of the group.

Don't just sign up "all the usual suspects" in going after leaders. Jesus went outside the religious establishment and invited a few "tax collectors and sinners" to join him in training. He found two on a fishing expedition, one at a tax collector's booth, and a "hothead" from the Zealots—hardly the places most would look for prospects.

Take your church membership list and check the names of everyone that you would like to invite to an information meeting about the future of your church. This should be used as an orientation meeting to explain the ministry and encourage people to take the leadership training. Ask God to lead you to the people in your church who at one time dropped out and have since returned. If you are going to reach out to prodigals, you will need to train prodigals who are on their way back to God.

Once you have decided on your "prospect list" for group leaders and apprentices, plan a 6-hour training session for these prospects.

The training session starts with an orientation by the pastor and leadership team to the program:

- the vision for this churchwide program
- how the program works—based on the Sunday Scripture and sermon
- when the program will begin
- how the groups will be organized
- how each group will start with three people and grow up to 12
- how groups can start with a short-term commitment and renew their commitment if they wish
- why the leadership in the group is easy because it is built around a handout with a 3-part agenda to guide the meeting

After this explanation of the program, divide into groups of 4 and run a practice session with the handout to show the prospects how easy it is to lead a group with the handout.

At the close of the training session, ask everyone to commit to being either: (1) group leader, (2) assistant / apprentice or (3) host for a small group. Remind the leaders that they will recruit the members of their group.

In addition to this initial training of leaders, it is best to meet with your small group leaders once a month to help troubleshoot where problems are occurring.

4. **Promote, Promote, Promote!** Promotion is the difference between whether "a good idea in theory" remains just "a good idea in theory" or becomes a vital part of a church's ministry. This kind of promotion has to be more than a couple of pulpit announcements and an article or two in the newsletter, although those are important. It has to include face-to-face promotion by you, the pastor. It has to include sermons on the importance of small groups to growth in discipleship and community. And it needs to include face-to-face recruitment of small group members by the small group leaders. Advertisers say repetition is the key to successfully promoting a product or event. Most people need to hear something at least six times before they really pay attention!

   WRITTEN ANNOUNCEMENTS IN THE CHURCH BULLETIN: Even better, put an insert in the bulletin that people can take home and put on their refrigerator. You could also include a card they can fill out and put in the offering plate if they are interested.

   VERBAL ANNOUNCEMENTS IN THE WORSHIP SERVICE: This is best when there is corresponding written information in the bulletin.

   BULLETIN BOARDS: If they are effective, use them! You could post a sign-up sheet.

   POSTERS: Placed strategically around the church, posters can be inexpensive, visual reminders for your program.

   DRAMA / SKITS: If your church is used to drama, this can be a powerful way to promote small groups in general, and your upcoming program in particular.

   VIDEO PRESENTATION: Videos can be a wonderful method of promoting events. Using either video or photographs, you can put together a video or slide presentation showing "real" people enjoying your small groups.

   PHONE TEAM: This is a fun job for your leaders, and other helpers, before your program starts. Meet at the church or someone's business after hours (where you have access to more than one line) and make a party out of it!

5. **Sign-Up Sundays.** For at least two Sundays people should be encouraged to sign up to be part of one of the groups. Remember, however, that this should not be the only way of enrolling group members. Group leaders should recruit personally from people in the church, as well as people in the community at large.

TAKE YOUR CHOICE OF GROUP
SUNDAY SCHOOL
SUNDAY NITE
WEEK NITE

When and How to Launch the Program

This program can start at the beginning of any season in the church year.

- ❒ ADVENT (6 weeks)—in December
- ❒ EPIPHANY / ORDINARY TIME (10 weeks)—in January
- ❒ LENT (6 weeks)—seven weeks to Easter
- ❒ EASTER (7 weeks)—from Easter to Pentecost
- ❒ FALL (12 weeks)—the last 12 weeks of Pentecost / Ordinary Time

If your church program follows the school year more than the church year in planning your calendar, you can easily structure this program into two semesters: (1) fall semester, and (2) spring semester. This would mean starting off with the last 12 weeks in the Pentecost season for your fall program and Epiphany for the winter program.

Another good season to start groups is Lent for six weeks, followed by Easter for the seven weeks leading up to Pentecost.

After you have decided on your kick-off season, here are the steps to follow:

Sign-Up Sundays. For at least two Sundays people should be encouraged to sign up to be part of one of the groups. Remember, however, that this should not be the only way of enrolling group members. Group leaders should recruit personally from people in the church, as well as people in the community at large.

1. **Ask for a 7-week commitment to groups.** Many people would be hesitant to sign up for a group that would go throughout the school year. Therefore, it's best to ask people to sign up for just a 7-week commitment.

2. **Renew contract / reopen groups after 7 weeks.** After the initial 7-week period, give people the chance to evaluate their involvement and either bow out or recommit. Also, this would be an excellent time to bring in new people to your groups.

3. **Take off for the summer.** This material is designed to not go through the summer. This gives people a break, and allows for a recommitment in the fall.

4. **Kick off the next fall.** Plan a special dinner, party or gathering to restart the groups next fall. Utilize the same promotional methods you used when you first started the program—face-to-face recruitment, coupled with pulpit announcements, newsletter articles, and two weeks for sign-up.

THESE ARE THE "GROUP RULES" —
ANY QUESTIONS? GOOD — LET'S BEGIN...
GROUP RULES

What Are the Ground Rules for Groups?

Unlike many of the group models which require a lot of skills for the leader, this program relies on a tight agenda and a guided questionnaire for conducting the group meetings.

Still, there are a few rules that need to be spelled out for this group. One of the best ways to help a group agree on the rules is to ask the group to fill in the blanks to these half-finished sentences at their first meeting.

PURPOSE: The purpose of this group is ...

DURATION: This group will last for _______ weeks, and then evaluate the experience before deciding to continue or not.

TIME: This group will meet from ____________ to ____________ and the meetings will begin on time and end on time.

EXPANSION: This group will keep an empty chair and aggressively seek to draw others into the group until it reaches ...

RULES: This group will agree to three or more of the following rules:

- ❑ **Priority:** While you are in the course, you give the group meetings priority.

- ❑ **Participation:** Everyone participates and no one dominates.

- ❑ **Respect:** Everyone is given the right to their own opinion, and all questions are encouraged and respected.

- ❑ **Confidentiality:** Anything shared in the meeting is never repeated outside of the meeting.

- ❑ **Empty Chair:** It will be the mission of this group to invite new people to the sessions. The group will be "open" to anyone who is struggling, and also to anyone who is seeking or who is starting over in the Christian life.

- ❑ **Support:** Permission is given to call upon each other in time of need at any time.

- ❑ **Advice-Giving:** It is okay to offer advice to another group member, but only when it is requested.

SMALL GROUP
CLINIC

How to Deal With Group Problems

Before you call the "repair technicians" at Serendipity, try these remedies for common group problems that arise:

1. **Exclusiveness.** Some groups feel that to be "close" (or to keep the discipline of confidentiality), they cannot allow new people in.

    Solution 1—Empty Chair. Remember the "empty chair" model where the group pulls up an empty chair into the group during the closing time, and consciously prays that God will fill that chair in the next meeting. The empty chair will be a constant reminder that your group is "open" to others.

    Solution 2—Rolling Covenants. To accomplish both the need to be "open" and the need to be "closed" (retain the closeness that fosters confidentiality), we recommend the strategy of rolling covenants. In the first 7-week covenant period of the group, the first four sessions are open and the last three sessions are closed to new people. Then, if the group wishes to renew their covenant for seven more weeks, the group is open again for the first four sessions of that time also, and closed for the last three sessions. This would continue throughout the life of the group.

2. **Shyness.** Some people clam up in groups and can't share, while others tend to talk too much or overwhelm the shy person.

    Solution: The Fearless Foursome. Subdivide into groups of no more than 4 persons when the time comes for sharing. In 4s, the quiet person will feel more relaxed, and the talkative person will not dominate as much. In fact, in 4s most of the problems of group dynamics are automatically avoided. It is best not to keep the same groups of 4 for every meeting, but rather reshuffle, so that everybody gets to know everyone else.

3. **Superficiality.** Too often small groups avoid deep sharing by staying on a head-to-head level. Even good Bible study can become a substitute for real sharing and real caring.

    *Solution 1—*Group leaders should make sure people answer the questions as written. Some questions early in the session are written for more of a "fun" response. But as you go farther into the sessions, the questions call for relating your own feelings or life experience. If group members try to circumvent this by making generalizations about what "people in general" do, get them back to what the questions ask for.

Solution 2—Save the last 20–40 minutes of the group time for CARING and have a timekeeper call time and regather the total group for a time of prayer requests and caring time at the close.

4. **Dominator.** What do you do when one person with special needs, or just a compulsion to talk too much, dominates the group?

   Solution: As the leader of the group, try to sit next to this person (where you can touch them when they begin to talk too long) or across from them (where you can use hand signals to slow them down) or take your eyes off this person and look down at your handout. If necessary, speak to the person after the meeting and review the ground rules; i.e., the purpose of this group and the need to follow the agenda. If the person persists, the group leader should call the pastor or small group overseer.

5. **Advice-Giving.** The unpardonable sin in any group (but one we all commit) is advice giving. We think we are helping a person who shares a need by telling them what to do. This often puts up a barrier in the group if this person does not "take the advice" or worse, takes the advice and it doesn't work.

   Solution: Learn how to share your own "story" about your own experience in that situation without giving advice. Start off with the word "I"—"I went through a time like that and I ... ." This is called sending an "I" message.

6. **Bad Meeting.** Every group will have a "bad" meeting every now and then. Very often a bad meeting is caused by not following the ground rules, or getting sidetracked into a theological argument.

   Solution: Admit it when you have a bad meeting. Learn from it. Be honest with the group and try to make sure that what caused it does not happen again. Here are typical causes of a bad meeting:

   • not starting on time
   • jumping into the Bible study without letting people "unpack"
   • letting the Bible study run too long and not giving the time for prayer requests and prayer at the close
   • getting too large and not breaking into groups of 4 for the Bible study
   • letting someone take over the meeting and ride their "hobbyhorse"

7. **Group Burnout.** What do you do when the group gets stale and some of the people start dropping out? The real problem here is burnout. This happens when a group has no purpose, no sense that what it is doing is still vital.

   Solution: Before the group gets underway, set the ground rules for the group (including the 7-week start), with a new covenant if the group wants to continue for another period beyond that. Also, remember the need for outreach and starting new groups. The natural result of a loving marriage relationship is children. The natural result of a loving group is new groups. Groups that hold on to each other exclusively will burn-out. Groups that give up their life together will give birth to many generations.

8. **Leadership.** The number one reason why small groups fail in the church is the failure of leadership on one of three levels:

   1. Pastoral level
   2. Management level
   3. Group leader training

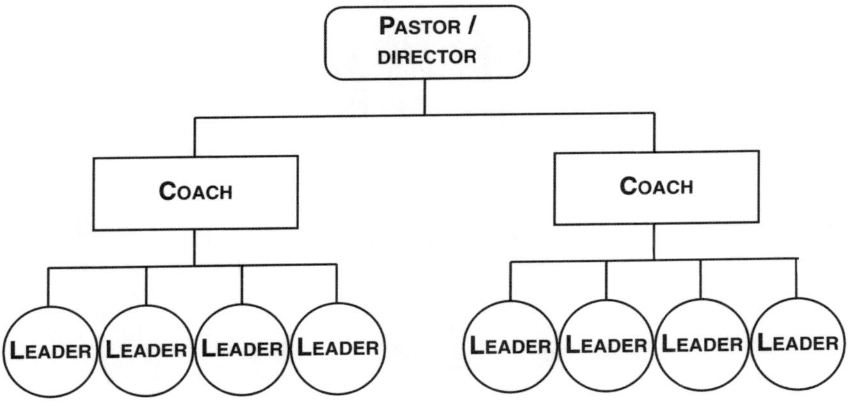

Solution: Monthly On-going Meetings. Build a leadership team to look after the group leaders. Recruit a set of coaches—with a coach for every five group leaders. Schedule a meeting once a month before or after church for group leaders—where they can get together with their coaches and talk about any problems. At the monthly meeting, the Pastor/Director of the program has the last 15 minutes with the whole group to review the big picture:

   - the "empty chair" principle of growing a group
   - the rolling covenant—renewing the covenant every 7 weeks
   - subdividing into groups of 4 for Bible study—when the group gets over 7
   - focusing on the CARING TIME—the last 30 minutes—for group members to share prayer requests and pray for one another

FALL SEASON
ADVENT & CHRISTMAS

Theme: "Signs of the Kingdom"

Small Group
HANDOUT

WEEK 1: ADVENT 1

Interrupting the Normal
Matthew 24:36–44

 **GATHERING**
10 min.

 **STUDY**
30 min.

 **CARING**
20–40 min.

Leader: The agenda has three parts. In the Gathering time you'll be getting to know each other through an "ice-breaker." This will be for your total group. The Study time has two parts: (1) Story and (2) Scripture. If you are short of time, skip the Story and move to the Scripture. Begin by reading out loud the Story or the Scripture to the whole group. Then divide into groups of 4 for the Study time. Finally, regather the total group for the Caring time. Keep to this agenda: (1) Gathering—10 minutes, (2) Study—30 minutes, and (3) Caring—20–40 minutes.

 **This Is Your Life!** On the classic television show, *This Is Your Life!* they used to take ordinary people and fly in significant people from their past to share things about the person's life. Well, congratulations! You have been selected for our version of the show—except you have to tell us who the most significant person was from each of the following periods of your life, and what that person might say you were like at that point in time. Have each person in the group take their turn in this exercise. If time is limited, you may want to have each person choose just two periods of their life:

GRADE SCHOOL: The person was__________________ who would say____.

HIGH SCHOOL: The person was__________________ who would say____.

COLLEGE / EARLY CAREER: The person was __________________ who would say ____.

<table>
<tr><td>

SESSION

1

</td><td>

Interrupting the Normal
Advent 1 - Matthew 24:36–44

</td></tr>
</table>

PURPOSE

To show how the signs of God's way come to us, interrupting our normal routines, bringing new direction to our life.

FOR THE PASTOR

The following material you can use as input for your sermon preparation on this week's Gospel Scripture from the book of Matthew. For further input you may want to share and further comment on the story of St. Francis of Assisi, which your study group(s) will be responding to during their session. Also, it's important to share in your sermon or homily your own response to the personal question (or other personally-oriented question) to model personal sharing for your congregation.

SCRIPTURE

36 "But about that day and hour no one knows, neither the angels of heaven, nor the Son, but only the Father. 37 For as the days of Noah were, so will be the coming of the Son of Man. 38 For as in those days before the flood they were eating and drinking, marrying and giving in marriage, until the day Noah entered the ark, 39 and they knew nothing until the flood came and swept them all away, so too will be the coming of the Son of Man. 40 Then two will be in the field; one will be taken and one will be left. 41 Two women will be grinding meal together; one will be taken and one will be left. 42 Keep awake therefore, for you do not know on what day your Lord is coming. 43 But understand this: if the owner of the house had known in what part of the night the thief was coming, he would have stayed awake and would not have let his house be broken into. 44 Therefore you also must be ready, for the Son of Man is coming at an unexpected hour."

Matthew 24:36–44

INTRODUCTION

Advent is a time for keeping watch. For centuries, the people of Israel had been warned to keep watch for the Messiah. Still, when he came as a baby in Bethlehem he caught people off guard. Now again today we are told to keep watch for Christ's coming into our midst. Primarily the warning is to watch for his second coming. But in another sense we are warned that Christ always comes to us in the midst of our normal routines, which is precisely the time we least expect it. That is how he came to Saint Francis. He came to a wealthy man who was neither better or worse than those around him—just living his normal life. But in the normality of routine, God's presence and call can be hidden.

24:36 *no one knows.* While scripture speaks of "signs" of the end time, this passage is explicit in declaring that only God knows when the end will come, and hence speaks against those who would try to make exact predictions.

24:37 *as the days of Noah were.* The emphasis here seems to be on the fact that most of the people during Moses' time were unaware of the coming catastrophe, and so people at the end of time would be unaware that judgment was coming. According to *The Interpreter's Bible,* "It was believed that events of Moses' time, such as the manna miracle, would be repeated in the messianic age, and that the age to come would be like the Garden of Eden; hence it was natural that the judgment should be thought of as striking as in the days of Noah."[1]

24:38–39 There is no condemnation of the activities here. The point is that the people were occupied with the daily routines of life right up to the actual time of God's judgment.

24:40–41 *one will be taken.* Some Christians use this verse to support a "rapture" of believers taken up to meet the Lord at his return. However, in light of the parallelism with the flood, it is more likely that what is meant here is that these people will, like those in Noah's time, be taken away in judgment. The people left are those, like Noah, who remained faithful to God.

24:43–44 The comparison of the Son of Man coming unexpectedly like a thief in the night is also found in 1 Thessalonians 5:2; 2 Peter 3:10 and Revelation 3:3; 16:15.

The members of your small groups will be responding to a variety of questions in their sharing time in relationship to the Scripture text as well as to the story. The first of these questions is generally a lighter question asking them to share from their own personal experience. As an example to your groups you may want to give your own response to this question during your sermon or at some other time. Here is the question for this week:

What has recently happened to you that has taken you completely by surprise?

STORY | **The Youth of Saint Francis of Assisi.** Saint Francis of Assisi is one of the great figures of faith in church history. He was a man who gave up wealth and privilege, took on the garb of the poor, and went across the country caring for the poor and building churches. He was a strong witness against a medieval church that had become materialistic, corrupt and indifferent to the poor. But before he was called to this life and witness, he lived the normal life of the wealthy. One biographer, Julien Green, describes it:

"Francis took up ... his favorite role of master of the revels, the leader, the dominus. It was so easy. People liked him, they felt his charm, and then—a somewhat disagreeable fact—there was the magic of money. The clothier's son knew how to turn his father's cash into handsome presents. He had style, enough to pass (with a little indulgence) for someone to the manner born. The good-looking little plebeian was never vulgar, and his elegance became proverbial among his contemporaries, as did his inexhaustible high spirits and his jokes that unleashed hysterical laughter. Obviously it all went to his head, knowing how admired he was for his wit, for his silk capes that were always new and surprising, and for his skill at ordering a dinner so fine a prince might envy it. He wanted to dazzle, and he also wanted everyone to enjoy themselves. On warm spring nights the tale was set in the open air. The guests ate ravenously, with the gluttony that marked the age, because however noble they might be, they had a monstrous appetite, all the more on account of the restrictions hard times had imposed on the aristocracy. They drank a lot and sang. The prettiest women in town were invited. ..."[2]

[1] From *The Interpreter's Bible*, ed. George Buttrick, Vol. 7: New Testament Articles—Matthew and Mark (Nashville: Abingdon Press, 1951), p. 552.
[2] Julien Green, *God's Fool: The Life and Times of Francis of Assisi* (San Francisco: Harper & Row, 1983), p. 38.

Small Group
HANDOUT

WEEK 2: ADVENT 2
Signs of Warning
Matthew 3:1–12

 **GATHERING**
10 min.

 **STUDY**
30 min.

 **CARING**
20–40 min.

Leader: The agenda has three parts. In the Gathering time you'll be getting to know each other through an "ice-breaker." This will be for your total group. The Study time has two parts: (1) Story and (2) Scripture. If you are short of time, skip the Story and move to the Scripture. Begin by reading out loud the Story or the Scripture to the whole group. Then divide into groups of 4 for the Study time. Finally, regather the total group for the Caring time. Keep to this agenda: (1) Gathering—10 minutes, (2) Study—30 minutes, and (3) Caring—20–40 minutes.

 **Life Signs.** Go around on question 1 and let everyone share. Then go around again on question 2.

1. If you were to select a traffic sign to tell how you've been seeking to live your life, what sign would it be?
   - ❒ "Merge"—because I've been trying to get along with everyone
   - ❒ "Keep Right"—because I'm trying to stay on the right track
   - ❒ "One Way"—because I am seeking to be more decisive in my life direction
   - ❒ "Yield"—because I'm seeking to yield my life to God
   - ❒ "Under Construction"—because I'm changing so much

2. If God were to give you a "traffic ticket" right now for how you are living your life, what would it be for?
   - ❒ "Speeding"—not slowing down enough to really live
   - ❒ "Failing to Yield"—trying to do things my own way
   - ❒ "Illegal U-Turn"—I have been trying to live in the past.
   - ❒ "Driving the Wrong Way on a One-Way Street"—I need to turn my life around.

Signs of Warning
Advent 2 - Matthew 3:1–12

PURPOSE

To look at some of the signs of warning that God brings into our life to point us away from death and toward life.

FOR THE PASTOR

The following material you can use as input for your sermon preparation on this week's Gospel Scripture from the book of Matthew. For further input you may want to share and further comment on the story of St. Augustine, which your study group(s) will be responding to during their session. Also, it's important to share in your sermon or homily your own response to the personal question (or other personally-oriented question) to model personal sharing for your congregation.

SCRIPTURE

3 *In those days John the Baptist appeared in the wilderness of Judea, proclaiming,* *2"Repent, for the kingdom of heaven has come near."* *3This is the one of whom the prophet Isaiah spoke when he said:*

> *"The voice of one crying out in the wilderness:*
> *'Prepare the way of the Lord,*
> *make his paths straight.' "*

4Now John wore clothing of camel's hair with a leather belt around his waist, and his food was locusts and wild honey. 5Then the people of Jerusalem and all Judea were going out to him, and all the region along the Jordan, 6and they were baptized by him in the river Jordan, confessing their sins.

7But when he saw many Pharisees and Sadducees coming for baptism, he said to them, "You brood of vipers! Who warned you to flee from the wrath to come? 8Bear fruit worthy of repentance. 9Do not presume to say to yourselves, 'We have Abraham as our ancestor'; for I tell you, God is able from these stones to raise up children to Abraham. 10Even now the ax is lying at the root of the trees: every tree therefore that does not bear good fruit is cut down and thrown into the fire.

11"I baptize you with water for repentance, but one who is more powerful than I is coming after me; I am not worthy to carry his sandals. He will baptize you with the Holy Spirit and fire. 12His winnowing fork is in his hand, and he will clear his threshing floor and will gather his wheat into the granary; but the chaff he will burn with unquenchable fire."

Matthew 3:1–12

Most of us don't like being told what we should not do. As children whatever we are told not to do is often the thing we are most curious about, and that attitude often persists into adulthood. But growing and maturing depends in large part on our ability to take heed to the "signs of warning" that are placed before us. When we are driving our car, heeding those signs of warning can mean life or death to us and our passengers: "Do not pass"; "One Way—do not enter"; "No U-turn." But when we are living our life, we must also learn to deal with warning signs: "Cigarette smoking may be hazardous to your health"; "Do not take this medication while operating machinery." Spiritually, the Bible contains many warning signs too. If we are to find the way to life, we must learn to pay heed to those signs. We will look at these "signs of warning" in this session, and what they mean to us as we prepare to celebrate our Lord's coming.

3:1 *the wilderness of Judea.* This was the term used for an area located in the lower Jordan valley between Central Judea and the Dead Sea. This region was 10 to 15 miles wide and extended for nearly 60 miles. It was a desolate and blistering hot place consisting of jagged limestone precipices and sparse vegetation.

3:2 *Repent.* To repent is not just to feel sorry for what one has done. Rather, it is a call to make a moral "U-turn," turning away from the activities and attitudes which lead away from God, and pursuing instead those activities that lead one toward God.

3:3 This is a quote from Isaiah 40:3. ***Prepare the way.*** Ancient roads were notoriously bad. The only time they tended to be smoothed out was in preparation for a royal visit.

3:4 This was the food eaten by the poorest of people.

3:6 *baptized.* There is no clear pre-Christian parallel to John's baptism, as other known types of baptism in that era were self-baptism. The Jewish sect at Qumran practiced frequent baptism as a cleansing from sin. Also, when Gentiles were converted to Judaism they were required to bathe in a river as part of the ceremony. John's call to baptism was a radical act highlighting that simply having the ethnic background of a Jew was no assurance of being one of God's people.

3:7 *Pharisees and Sadducees.* The Pharisees were a small but powerful religious sect of laymen who devoted their time, energy and money to a strict observance of the religious regulations of the law. The Pharisees often clashed with Jesus, but they were not all bad. Like Jesus, they believed in eternal life and accepted most of what we call the Old Testament as scriptural, in contrast to the Sadducees, who did not believe in eternal life, and who only accepted the first five books of the Old Testament (the Torah) as scriptural. ***You brood of vipers.*** The image painted by these words is of snakes slithering through the undergrowth trying to escape an oncoming fire. ***the wrath to come.*** The final judgment of God.

The members of your small groups will be responding to a variety of questions in their sharing time in relationship to the Scripture text as well as to the story below. The first of these questions is generally a lighter question asking them to share from their own personal experience. As an example to your groups you may want to give your own response to this question during your sermon or at some other time. Here is the question for this week:

When you were a teenager, what do you remember people warning you about that you consistently ignored?

The following story is included in the group participant leaflet. Group members will read and respond to the story as part of their study. It is included here because you may want to further comment on the story's relevance to the text, and because some who come for your sermon will not participate in the small groups, and may want to hear the story.

Augustine's Forbidden Fruit. Augustine was one of the church's first great intellects. His *Confessions* is called by some "the greatest spiritual autobiography of all time." In it he tells of his own conversion from what he later considered to be a rather sinful life, that included fathering a child out of wedlock. But one incident that many would consider minor seemed to greatly disturb his conscience, and that was a time when he joined some friends in pilfering some fruit from a neighbor's tree. He writes of this incident:

"Surely, Lord, your law punishes theft, as does that law written on the hearts of men, which not even iniquity itself blots out. What thief puts up with another thief with a calm mind? Not even a rich thief will pardon one who steals from him because of want. But I willed to commit theft, and I did so, not because I was driven to it by any need, unless it were by poverty of justice, and dislike of it, and by a glut of evil-doing. For I stole a thing of which I had plenty of my own and of much better quality. Nor did I wish to enjoy that thing which I desired to gain by theft, but rather to enjoy the actual theft and the sin of theft.

"In a garden nearby our vineyard there was a pear tree, loaded with fruit that was desirable neither in appearance nor in taste. Late one night—to which hour, according to our pestilential custom, we had kept up our street games—a group of very bad youngsters set out to shake down and rob this tree. We took great loads of fruit from it, not for our own eating, but rather to throw it to the pigs; even if we did eat a little of it, we did this to do what pleased us for the reason that it was forbidden. ..."[1]

[1] John K. Ryan, Translator *The Confessions of St. Augustine* (New York: Doubleday, 1960), pp. 69–70.

SERENDIPITY

Small Group
H A N D O U T

WEEK 3: ADVENT 3

Signs of Healing
Matthew 11:2–11

 **GATHERING**
10 min.

 **STUDY**
30 min.

 **CARING**
20–40 min.

Leader: The agenda has three parts. In the Gathering time you'll be getting to know each other through an "ice-breaker." This will be for your total group. The Study time has two parts: (1) Story and (2) Scripture. If you are short of time, skip the Story and move to the Scripture. Begin by reading out loud the Story or the Scripture to the whole group. Then divide into groups of 4 for the Study time. Finally, regather the total group for the Caring time. Keep to this agenda: (1) Gathering—10 minutes, (2) Study—30 minutes, and (3) Caring—20–40 minutes.

 **The Real Me or an Impostor?** A common theme in many spy or action movies is where the bad guys have performed surgery on someone, so that he or she looks exactly like the hero. Then the counterfeit person commits all these crimes and the hero gets blamed! Well, to protect ourselves against just that sort of scenario, respond to the following items, so we know how to differentiate between the fake and the real you:

You will know it's the impostor if ...

- ❒ I refuse dessert.
- ❒ I volunteer to pray aloud.
- ❒ I drink the decaffeinated coffee.
- ❒ I'm agreeing with the president.
- ❒ I'm wearing a tie.
- ❒ I arrive on time.
- ❒ I'm wearing a dress.
- ❒ other:_____________
- ❒ I can't tell you what happened in my favorite soap opera.
- ❒ I don't know what the stock market did today.
- ❒ I don't know what my favorite team did recently.
- ❒ I volunteer to read the Bible passage.
- ❒ I agree to go shopping with someone.
- ❒ I say something like "I hope the children are still up when we get home."

Signs of Healing
Advent 3 - Matthew 11:2–11

PURPOSE

To learn to recognize the signs God gives us that he is offering healing for our brokenness.

FOR THE PASTOR

The following material you can use as input for your sermon preparation on this week's Gospel Scripture from the book of Matthew. For further input you may want to share and further comment on the story of Thomas Merton, which your study group(s) will be responding to during their session. Also, it's important to share in your sermon or homily your own response to the personal question (or other personally-oriented question) to model personal sharing for your congregation.

SCRIPTURE

²When John heard in prison what the Messiah was doing, he sent word by his disciples ³and said to him, "Are you the one who is to come, or are we to wait for another?" ⁴Jesus answered them, "Go and tell John what you hear and see: ⁵the blind receive their sight, the lame walk, the lepers are cleansed, the deaf hear, the dead are raised, and the poor have good news brought to them. ⁶And blessed is anyone who takes no offense at me."

⁷As they went away, Jesus began to speak to the crowds about John: "What did you go out into the wilderness to look at? A reed shaken by the wind? ⁸What then did you go out to see? Someone dressed in soft robes? Look, those who wear soft robes are in royal palaces. ⁹What then did you go out to see? A prophet? Yes, I tell you, and more than a prophet. ¹⁰This is the one about whom it is written:

> *" 'See, I am sending my messenger ahead of you,*
> *who will prepare your way before you.'*

¹¹Truly I tell you, among those born of women no one has arisen greater than John the Baptist; yet the least in the kingdom of heaven is greater than he."

Matthew 11:2–11

INTRODUCTION

Many of us go through life seeking some kind of healing—not necessarily physical healing, but emotional and spiritual healing. Perhaps as a child we were always put down, or perhaps our parents divorced or one of them died, or maybe we felt rejected by our peers. Even many of us who had a relatively happy childhood, have since then had traumatic events happen to us, from which we need healing. For many of us, while "signs of warning" are important in showing us what to avoid, "signs of healing" are what we really seek and are drawn to. Where in this world can we go to heal our soul? For those seeking such signs, Advent is a time of hope. It is significant that Christmas comes at the darkest time of the year, when the hours of night are the longest. But from Christmas on the days get longer, and the world is brighter. So it is that in the coming of Christ we celebrate the coming of light to our darkness and healing to our souls.

11:2–3 *in prison.* According to Josephus (a Jewish historian), Herod had imprisoned John in the fortress of Machaerus on the east side of the Dead Sea. He arrested John at the instigation of his wife Herodias who was angry at John for denouncing their marriage (see 14:1–12). ***Are you the one who is to come ...?*** The one who was to come was another title for the Messiah (Hebrew) or Christ (Greek). Apparently John had expected a different sort of Messiah. Jesus' ministry thus far is not what John described in 3:11–12.

11:5 Jesus' response is in terms drawn from Isaiah 29:18–19; 35:5–6 and 61:1.

11:6 The Jews of this time expected a militaristic Messiah. With that kind of expectation, they may have been put off by Jesus' gentler, more healing ministry.

11:7–8 Jesus' words at this point may have drawn some smiles, because anyone who knew John would know these words would not describe him. He was a rough-hewn character who was definitely not a weak and vacillating reed swayed by every kind of opinion. Even less could he be described as someone dressed in soft robes—his clothes were made of camel's hair! (Matt. 3:4).

11:9–10 John's role, as the quotation from Malachi 3:1 shows, was to prepare for the coming of the Messiah.

11:11 John was the best part of the old order. He would not be part of Jesus' ministry and new way. This does not mean he wouldn't find salvation, any more than one would deny salvation to Old Testament saints.

Jesus pointed to John the Baptist as the greatest person of his era. Who would you say was the greatest person in terms of his or her effect on you and your life when you were a teenager?

The Recovery of Thomas Merton. Thomas Merton was a great Christian mystic, whose autobiography, *The Seven Storey Mountain,* traces his spiritual journey from his childhood in a religiously apathetic family to his becoming part of a Trappist monastery. With his mother and father both dead, he spent his youth in a search for what life is about. A serious illness which came as a result of blood poisoning from an infection, seemed later to symbolize for him a greater spiritual illness or lethargy. His recovery from that illness was in some respects the beginning of his own spiritual recovery. He describes that time of illness in this way:

"The room was very quiet. It was rather dark, too. And as I lay in bed, in my weariness and pain and disgust, I felt for a moment the shadow of another visitor pass into the room.

"It was death, that came to stand by my bed.

"I kept my eyes closed, more out of apathy than anything else. But anyway, there was no need to open one's eyes to see the visitor, to see death. Death is someone you see very clearly with eyes in the center of your heart: eyes that see not by reacting to light, but by reacting to a kind of chill from within the marrow of your own life.

"And, with those eyes, those interior eyes, open upon that coldness, I lay half asleep and looked at the visitor, death.

"What did I think? All I remember was that I was filled with a deep and tremendous apathy. I felt so sick and disgusted that I did not very much care whether I died or lived. ...

"But at any rate, I lay there in a kind of torpor and said: 'Come on, I don't care.' And then I fell asleep.

"What a tremendous mercy it was that death did not take me at my word, that day, when I was still only seventeen years old. ...

"... I wish I could give those who believe in God some kind of an idea of the state of a soul like mine was in then. But it is impossible to do it in sober, straight, measured, prose terms. ... But my soul was simply dead. It was a blank, a nothingness. ..."[1]

Small Group
H A N D O U T

WEEK 4: ADVENT 4
Signs of God's Presence
Matthew 1:18–25

 **GATHERING**
10 min.

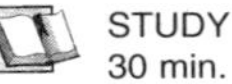 **STUDY**
30 min.

 **CARING**
20–40 min.

Leader: The agenda has three parts. In the Gathering time you'll be getting to know each other through an "ice-breaker." This will be for your total group. The Study time has two parts: (1) Story and (2) Scripture. If you are short of time, skip the Story and move to the Scripture. Begin by reading out loud the Story or the Scripture to the whole group. Then divide into groups of 4 for the Study time. Finally, regather the total group for the Caring time. Keep to this agenda: (1) Gathering—10 minutes, (2) Study—30 minutes, and (3) Caring—20–40 minutes.

 **Pictures of My Family.** Select a movie or a fairy tale which best describes your family of origin. Tell your group what you have chosen and feel free to explain your selections.

IF MY FAMILY OF ORIGIN WERE A MOVIE, IT WOULD'VE BEEN ...

- ❏ Nightmare on Elm Street
- ❏ The Parent Trap
- ❏ It's a Wonderful Life
- ❏ Sleeping With the Enemy
- ❏ Ordinary People
- ❏ What's Love Got to Do With It?
- ❏ The Joy Luck Club
- ❏ Parenthood
- ❏ Rambo
- ❏ Aladdin
- ❏ Home Alone
- ❏ Star Wars
- ❏ Places in the Heart

IF MY FAMILY OF ORIGIN WERE A FAIRY TALE, IT WOULD'VE BEEN ...

- ❏ Hansel and Gretel
- ❏ Jack and the Beanstalk
- ❏ Cinderella
- ❏ Sleeping Beauty
- ❏ Beauty and the Beast
- ❏ The Emperor's New Clothes
- ❏ The Pied Piper
- ❏ Goldilocks & the Three Bears

<table>
<tr><td>

SESSION
4

</td><td>

Signs of God's Presence
Advent 4 - Matthew 1:18–25

</td></tr>
</table>

PURPOSE

To learn to see the signs of God's presence in our world, so we can be an active participant with him in what he is doing.

FOR THE PASTOR

The following material you can use as input for your sermon preparation on this week's Gospel Scripture from the book of Matthew. For further input you may want to share and further comment on the story of Thomas Merton, which your study group(s) will be responding to during their session. Also, it's important to share in your sermon or homily your own response to the personal question (or other personally-oriented question) to model personal sharing for your congregation.

SCRIPTURE

[18]Now the birth of Jesus the Messiah took place in this way. When his mother Mary had been engaged to Joseph, but before they lived together, she was found to be with child from the Holy Spirit. [19]Her husband Joseph, being a righteous man and unwilling to expose her to public disgrace, planned to dismiss her quietly. [20]But just when he had resolved to do this, an angel of the Lord appeared to him in a dream and said, "Joseph, son of David, do not be afraid to take Mary as your wife, for the child conceived in her is from the Holy Spirit. [21]She will bear a son, and you are to name him Jesus, for he will save his people from their sins." [22]All this took place to fulfill what had been spoken by the Lord through the prophet:

> **[23]"Look, the virgin shall conceive and bear a son,**
>   **and they shall name him Emmanuel,"**

which means, "God is with us." [24]When Joseph awoke from sleep, he did as the angel of the Lord commanded him; he took her as his wife, [25]but had no marital relations with her until she had borne a son; and he named him Jesus.

Matthew 1:18–25

INTRODUCTION

The story is told of a little girl who couldn't sleep because of a storm, and so she called her mother into her room. The mother stayed with her a while, and then sought to go. When the little girl resisted, the mother said, "You know, honey, God will be right here with you." The little girl responded, "I know, Mommy. But I want somebody with skin on them!" So it is that Jesus came into the world to be "God with skin on," and to be a reassuring presence in our world. While even Jesus is no longer here in the flesh, we who follow in Christ's steps become his presence, and therefore, God's presence, to each other, and to those who have yet to meet Christ. We need to be God's presence for those who are scared, for those who are lonely and for those who are experiencing the injustice of the world. Advent must be a time for us when we are reminded how God came to be present with us, and how we are to put some flesh on his presence today.

1:18 *engaged.* A first century Jewish marriage had three parts to it: the engagement (which often took place when the couple were children and which was usually arranged by a marriage broker); the betrothal (a one-year period in which the couple were considered virtually married, though they did not have sexual relations); and the marriage. ***she was found to be with child.*** The law's penalty for sleeping with a woman betrothed to another was death by stoning for both parties (Deut. 22:23–24). By this time, however, the breaking of the engagement was the course that was normally followed.

1:19 By law, Joseph was required to break off his relationship with Mary (Deut. 24:1). However, out of compassion for her he decided not to do this publicly. ***Her husband.*** Although the marriage had not yet taken place, a betrothed couple were considered to be husband and wife. ***dismiss.*** During betrothal, a divorce was required should either party wish to break off the relationship. ***quietly.*** To break off his engagement privately he would have needed only two witnesses.

1:20–21 *take Mary as your wife.* The marriage was completed when the husband took his betrothed from her parents' home where she lived during the betrothal to his own home. Joseph needed to marry Mary in order for Jesus to become his legal son and share his lineage back to David. ***to name him.*** It was necessary for Joseph to name Jesus and thus formally accept him as his son. ***Jesus.*** A common name. It is the Greek form of the Hebrew name Joshua, which meant "God is salvation."

1:23 *God is with us.* The allusion is to Isaiah 7:14. The presence of God with his people is the climactic promise of God's covenant with Israel.

1:24–25 The marriage was completed, though not consummated until after the birth of Jesus.

Do you know how your parents picked your name? What does your name mean?

The Sensing of God's Presence. In the last session we looked at Thomas Merton, whose autobiography, *The Seven Storey Mountain,* traces his spiritual journey from his childhood in a religiously apathetic family to his becoming part of a Trappist monastery. In the following section of his story, he tells of a time he especially sensed God's presence in worship. In Merton's case, his worship was within a Catholic context, and some of the concepts are uniquely Catholic, but the basic experience has a universality to it. Here is how it was for Thomas Merton:

"I was in the Church of St. Francis at Havana. It was Sunday. ... The building was crowded. Up in front before the altar, there were rows and rows of children, crowded together. ...

"It came time for the Consecration. The priest raised the Host and then he raised the chalice. When he put the chalice down on the altar, suddenly a Friar in his brown robe and white cord stood up in front of the children, and all at once the voices of the children burst out:

" 'Creo en Dios. ...'

" 'I believe in God the Father Almighty, The creator of heaven and earth. ...'

"The Creed. But that cry, 'Creo en Dios!' It was loud and bright and sudden and glad and triumphant; it was a good big shout, that came from all those Cuban children, a joyful affirmation of faith.

"Then as sudden as the shout and as definite, and a thousand times more bright, there formed in my mind an awareness, an understanding, a realization of what had just taken place on the altar, at the Consecration: a realization of God made present by the words of Consecration in a way that made Him belong to me.

"But what a thing it was, this awareness: it was so intangible, and yet it struck me like a thunderclap. It was a light that was so bright that it had no relation to any visible light and so profound and so intimate that it seemed like a neutralization of every lesser experience. ...

"It was as if I had been suddenly illuminated by being blinded by the manifestation of God's presence."[1]

[1]Thomas Merton, *The Seven Storey Mountain* , pp. 315–316. © Harcourt, Brace & Company. All rights reserved.

WEEK 5: CHRISTMAS 1

Signs of God's Protection
Matthew 2:13–23

 **GATHERING**
10 min.

 **STUDY**
30 min.

 **CARING**
20–40 min.

Leader: The agenda has three parts. In the Gathering time you'll be getting to know each other through an "ice-breaker." This will be for your total group. The Study time has two parts: (1) Story and (2) Scripture. If you are short of time, skip the Story and move to the Scripture. Begin by reading out loud the Story or the Scripture to the whole group. Then divide into groups of 4 for the Study time. Finally, regather the total group for the Caring time. Keep to this agenda: (1) Gathering—10 minutes, (2) Study—30 minutes, and (3) Caring—20–40 minutes.

 **Guardians of the Group.** There are many kinds of guardians in the world that protect us from danger. This group has had its "guardians," too. In silence decide which person in the group best fulfilled each of the following roles for you. Then, focus on one group member at a time, and have the others report the role they chose for that person.

POLICE OFFICER: the one who protected us from our own unruliness

HEART MONITOR: the one who kept the group alive by keeping in touch with the heart

TRAIL GUIDE: the one who kept us on the right path

CLASS CLOWN: the one who lightened heavy stuff through humor

"CHILD" WHO GUIDES US TO THE KINGDOM: the one who protected our innocence and childlike faith

GUARDIAN ANGEL: the one whose loving protection seemed to come from God

MOTHER HEN: the one who took us in like her own children

<table>
<tr><td>SESSION

5</td><td><h1>Signs of God's Protection</h1>
Christmas 1 - Matthew 2:13–23</td></tr>
</table>

PURPOSE

To consider the signs God has given us that he will be there for us in times of stress, watching over us.

FOR THE PASTOR

The following material you can use as input for your sermon preparation on this week's Gospel Scripture from the book of Matthew. For further input you may want to share and further comment on the story of St. Francis of Assisi, which your study group(s) will be responding to during their session. Also, it's important to share in your sermon or homily your own response to the personal question (or other personally-oriented question) to model personal sharing for your congregation.

SCRIPTURE

[13]Now after they had left, an angel of the Lord appeared to Joseph in a dream and said, "Get up, take the child and his mother, and flee to Egypt, and remain there until I tell you; for Herod is about to search for the child, to destroy him." [14]Then Joseph got up, took the child and his mother by night, and went to Egypt, [15]and remained there until the death of Herod. This was to fulfill what had been spoken by the Lord through the prophet, "Out of Egypt I have called my son."

[16]When Herod saw that he had been tricked by the wise men, he was infuriated, and he sent and killed all the children in and around Bethlehem who were two years old or under, according to the time that he had learned from the wise men. [17]Then was fulfilled what had been spoken through the prophet Jeremiah:

[18]   "A voice was heard in Ramah,
*   wailing and loud lamentation,*
*   Rachel weeping for her children;*
*   she refused to be consoled,*
*   because they are no more."*

[19]When Herod died, an angel of the Lord suddenly appeared in a dream to Joseph in Egypt and said, [20]"Get up, take the child and his mother, and go to the land of Israel, for those who were seeking the child's life are dead." [21]Then Joseph got up, took the child and his mother, and went to the land of Israel. [22]But when he heard that Archelaus was ruling over Judea in place of his father Herod, he was afraid to go there. And after being warned in a dream, he went away to the district of Galilee. [23]There he made his home in a town called Nazareth, so that what had been spoken through the prophets might be fulfilled, "He will be called a Nazorean."

Matthew 2:13–23

It does not take great powers of observation to see that we live in a dangerous world. Child abductions, drive-by shootings, and acts of terrorism are becoming a disturbingly regular part of our lives. Even in small cities and towns, which we used to think of as exempt from such dangers, we find these dangers creeping in, often shocking people out of their previous sense of security. What can be done? Some people build big fences and install home security systems, but at what point does walling out others become walling ourselves in? None of us can totally eliminate the danger in our lives. All we can do is put ourselves in God's hands. Putting ourselves in God's hands will not assure us that we will never be victimized by the world's violence. After all, that even happened to God's Son! But what it does mean is that whatever happens, God will help us through it, and in the end we will have the victory. For not even death itself can separate us from the love of God in Christ Jesus (Rom. 8:35–39)! Advent is the time when we celebrate the coming into the world of the one who brought us this kind of security.

2:13 *Egypt.* There were large colonies of Jews in Egypt and it would have been easy enough for Mary, Joseph and the child to lose themselves there.

2:15 *until the death of Herod.* Herod died in 4 B.C. Given this fact as well as the fact that Herod ordered all children under 2 years of age to be killed, it is probable that Jesus was born between 7 and 5 B.C. (The B.C./A.D. dating system was not developed until centuries later, and the calculations were slightly off.) ***Out of Egypt.*** According to *The Interpreter's Bible,* "Early Christians often thought of the Exodus with its miracles as a type of Christian redemption."[1]

2:16 *two years old.* This seems to indicate that some time had elapsed since Jesus' actual birth. Herod wants to make sure the right child is killed. Probably 20 or 30 children were slaughtered in this village. That Herod was capable of such a barbarous act is made clear by the fact that near the time of his death he ordered the arrest of a number of leading people. They were to be executed at the time of his death in order to insure that there would be genuine mourning when he died!

2:17–18 As Rachel wept for her children (Jer. 31:15), so too did the mothers in Bethlehem. Interestingly, the context of the passage in Jeremiah is one of hope, so perhaps Matthew is suggesting that beyond this sorrow there lies the triumph which the Messiah will bring.

2:19–23 When Herod dies, Joseph is told in yet another dream that it is safe to return to the land of Israel (v. 20). A final dream (v. 22) warns him against returning to Judea.

2:22 *Archelaus.* When Herod died, his kingdom was divided into three parts. His eldest son Archelaus ruled as Governor of Judea, Idumea and Samaria. Archelaus was never confirmed in this post by the emperor Augustus, however, since he proved himself to be cruel and incompetent and so was removed in a few years. The implication of this section is that Joseph originally intended to return his family to Bethlehem. Some see this as being an alternative explanation as to why Jesus was born in Bethlehem, yet raised in Nazareth, to Luke's version that Joseph and his family only went to Bethlehem in the first place for a government-imposed census.

2:23 *a Nazorean.* While historically true that Jesus was from Nazareth, there is no Old Testament quote that predicts this. The reference here is probably from Judges 13:5, where the original reference was "The boy shall be a Nazirite," which refers to a person who takes a certain vows.

When was there a time in your own life when God's protection and direction steered you away from danger, or helped you out of danger?

Saint Francis and God's Provision. Saint Francis of Assisi grew up as a "spoiled rich kid." But there came a time when he decided to throw all of that away and give himself to God by identifying with and ministering to the poor. At first he used some of his father's resources to do what he saw as his ministry, selling some of his expensive cloth to get money to rebuild a poor little church at San Damiano. But his father was enraged by this, and took him before the bishop of Assisi to get the bishop to make Francis return the purse full of coins he had gotten for the cloth. Saint Francis' biographer, Julien Green, tells the story:

"A wise and prudent man, but deeply attached to the goods of this world, Monsignor Guido, the bishop of Assisi, formally summoned Francis. ... The prince of the Church received him with joy and delivered a short speech that was a model of tact and good sense. 'You have scandalized your father. If you wish to serve God, return to him the money that you possess. Perhaps it was ill-gotten ... and God does not want you to use it for sacred things. Have confidence, act like a man. As for San Damiano, God will provide. *Dominus providebit.*'

"There could have been no better way to transform Francis into an ardent soldier for Christ. His head was spinning a bit as he stood before the crowd of curious onlookers assembled to watch the scene in the public square, not far down from his father's house. ... Without a word he tore off his clothes in hot haste and threw them, one item after another, at his father's feet—everything including his breeches and, to top it off, the damned purse that he had simply brought with him, hidden in one of his pockets. Now he was naked as the day he was born. Naked today for his second birth.

"... Lunatics suffer from a compulsion to strip themselves naked, and he too felt like a lunatic, crazy with anger and love; and in a delirium of enthusiasm he cried out, with a master's authority: 'Listen, listen, everyone. From now on I can say with complete freedom, "Our Father who art in heaven." Pietro Bernardone is no longer my father, and I am giving him back not only his money—here it is—but all my clothes as well.' And the last words he shouted had the sound of the Magnificat, 'I shall go naked to meet the Lord.' "[2]

[1] From *The Interpreter's Bible,* ed. George Buttrick Vol. 7: New Testament Articles—Matthew and Mark (Nashville: Abingdon Press, 1951), p. 260.
[2] Julien Green, *God's Fool: The Life and Times of Francis of Assisi* (San Francisco: Harper & Row, 1985), pp. 81–83.

Small Group
HANDOUT

WEEK 6: CHRISTMAS 2

Signs of Family Resemblance
John 1:1–18

 **GATHERING**
10 min.

 **STUDY**
30 min.

 **CARING**
20–40 min.

Leader: The agenda has three parts. In the Gathering time you'll be getting to know each other through an "ice-breaker." This will be for your total group. The Study time has two parts: (1) Story and (2) Scripture. If you are short of time, skip the Story and move to the Scripture. Begin by reading out loud the Story or the Scripture to the whole group. Then divide into groups of 4 for the Study time. Finally, regather the total group for the Caring time. Keep to this agenda: (1) Gathering—10 minutes, (2) Study—30 minutes, and (3) Caring—20–40 minutes.

 **Like Music to My Ears.** Go around the group and have each person answer the question.

Which of each of the following pairs of sounds is most likely to be "like music to your ears"?

the crackling of a campfire	the sounds of city traffic at night
the cry of "play ball!"	waves crashing against the shore
the laughter of children	the laughter of an adult party
a train whistle in the distance	the bell of an ice cream truck
the ring of the telephone	the ring of a cash register
the gurgling of a mountain stream	the talk of an opening-night crowd
the purr of a kitten	the hum of a well-tuned engine
the silence of new fallen snow	the cheering of a crowd
the sound of gentle rain	the rapid talk of an auctioneer
the chirping of a bird	the crackling of a thunderstorm

Signs of Family Resemblance
Christmas 2 - John 1:1–18

PURPOSE

To see the "signs of family resemblance" between Jesus and God his Father, and the "resemblance" which should exist between us, Jesus and God.

FOR THE PASTOR

The following material you can use as input for your sermon preparation on this week's Gospel Scripture from the book of John. For further input you may want to share and further comment on the story of Mother Teresa, which your study group(s) will be responding to during their session. Also, it's important to share in your sermon or homily your own response to the personal question (or other personally-oriented question) to model personal sharing for your congregation.

SCRIPTURE

1 *In the beginning was the Word, and the Word was with God, and the Word was God. [2]He was in the beginning with God. [3]All things came into being through him, and without him not one thing came into being. What has come into being [4]in him was life, and the life was the light of all people. [5]The light shines in the darkness, and the darkness did not overcome it.*

[6]There was a man sent from God, whose name was John. [7]He came as a witness to testify to the light, so that all might believe through him. [8]He himself was not the light, but he came to testify to the light. [9]The true light, which enlightens everyone, was coming into the world.

[10]He was in the world, and the world came into being through him; yet the world did not know him. [11]He came to what was his own, and his own people did not accept him. [12]But to all who received him, who believed in his name, he gave power to become children of God, [13]who were born, not of blood or of the will of the flesh or of the will of man, but of God.

[14]And the Word became flesh and lived among us, and we have seen his glory, the glory as of a father's only son, full of grace and truth. [15](John testified to him and cried out, "This was he of whom I said, 'He who comes after me ranks ahead of me because he was before me.' ") [16]From his fullness we have all received, grace upon grace. [17]The law indeed was given through Moses; grace and truth came through Jesus Christ. [18]No one has ever seen God. It is God the only Son, who is close to the Father's heart, who has made him known.

John 1:1–18

"We Are Family" was a song by Sister Sledge that was popular back in the '70s. It was a celebrative song, and well it should have been, because to realize that we are not isolated, unconnected individuals in this world is great news! We don't have to face our struggles alone. When we have something to celebrate, we have others to celebrate with us. But this family connectedness is not ultimately a matter of biology. People born to the same parents can just as easily be rivals and antagonists, if they are not united in spirit. In the church, it is our relationship to God through Christ that unites us in spirit and makes us family. God shows his love to us through Christ in order to be united with us. We show that love to each other, and the family connection is complete. "But to all who received him [accepted his love], who believed in his name, he gave power to become children of God [a family united in love] (John 1:12)."

1:1 *In the beginning.* John's version of the "New Testament" begins with the same phrase that begins the Old Testament. This underlines the fact that the coming of Jesus inaugurates a new creation. ***the Word.*** This is the translation of the Greek word *Logos,* a word with multiple meanings from both Greek philosophy and the Old Testament.

1:4 *life.* This word also has a double meaning, referring to both physical life and the supernatural illumination that brings life to all people.

1:5 *light / darkness.* A Jewish sect called the Essenes, who separated themselves from the rest of Jewish society, had a book called, *The War of the Sons of Light Against the Sons of Darkness,* and this was apparently a popular theme of the day.

1:6 *John.* John the Baptist's influence was felt from Egypt to Asia Minor (Acts 18:24–26; 19:1–4). Some scholars think the emphasis on John's role as a witness to the coming of the Messiah was because, even after Jesus, many of John's followers still saw John as the Messiah.

1:11 *to what was his own.* Israel, God's own people (Gen. 17:7), especially failed to see who Jesus was. But in a larger sense, we are all "God's own" and have failed to see who Jesus was.

1:12 *power to become children of God.* In one sense we are all children of God from birth, for God created us all. But spiritually, when we rebel against God, we renounce our family and become children of the world. Only by finding forgiveness through Christ do we find power to become children of God again.

1:14 *the Word became flesh.* This is a repudiation of the doctrine of the Gnostics (a popular philosophy of the time), which disparaged humanity's physical nature, and said that Christ could not have really taken on human flesh, since flesh is inherently evil. "Flesh," while sometimes used by John in contrast to "spirit," does not carry any derogatory sense. ***and lived among us.*** The Greek word used for "lived" here literally meant "tented." John may have been thinking of the tabernacle in the wilderness where the Lord dwelt with Israel.

1:15 *he was before me.* The *Logos,* here identified with Christ, was seen as a preexistent agent of creation.

1:18 *who has made him known.* As a person can often see a child's parent in the child, so Christ, as the perfect child, perfectly reflected his Parent.

<table>
<tr><td>PERSONAL QUESTION</td><td>In what ways are you a "chip off the old block," looking or acting like your parents?</td></tr>
<tr><td>STORY</td><td>

Mother Teresa Expands Her Work. Most people know Mother Teresa as one who worked with "the poorest of the poor" in Calcutta, India. But many do not know of the expansion of her work into other parts of the world. Her biographer, Lush Gjergji, tells of a meeting with Mother Teresa at a new work she started in Rome. Catholic nuns are called "Sister" and "Mother," and of course the emphasis is that in Christ we are united as a family. Perhaps in no work is this family love seen more than in the work of Mother Teresa. Lush Gjergji describes her reaction:

"When I was a student in Rome I went with a few companions to visit the house and to greet Mother Teresa. ...

"It was a small, very poor house, like so many others around it. Fortunately, we found Mother Teresa there. ... I was amazed by the simplicity and the attention with which she listened to me. I found her a deeply thoughtful woman, with tiny body and hands, full of enthusiasm, a woman of deep convictions and burning love. When one was with her one had the impression of being outside of time and space; one felt tranquil, secure and happy, like a child close to its mother. So full of joy were we that we could not believe our good fortune. ...

"What was there to see? Nothing but the profoundest want. How often had I not passed by these shacks without ever noticing their sorry condition. There, not far away, the road leading to the Roman Castelli seemed to separate two different worlds. On one side the elegant, modern city, with its magnificent buildings (apparently magnificent, any way), while on the other side huts made of old planks, corrugated iron or cardboard marred the landscape. ...

"Right away I wrote down my impressions about meeting Mother Teresa. Here are some extracts:

" 'I cannot understand the simplicity, the love and the dedication Mother Teresa shows to the poor, nor can I grasp the peace of soul, the attention and the love she shared with us. She is a nun different from the rest. Different too is her lifestyle and that of her Sisters. How far we are from the gospel, while she is putting it into practice day by day as she lives among these people.' "[1]

</td></tr>
</table>

[1] Lush Gjergji, *Mother Teresa: Her Life, Her Works* (Hyde Park, NY: New City Press, 1991), pp. 86–88.

WINTER SEASON
EPIPHANY / ORDINARY TIME

Theme: "The Light of the World"

WEEK 1: EPIPHANY OF OUR LORD
A Guiding Light
Matthew 2:1–12

 **GATHERING** 10 min.  **STUDY** 30 min.  **CARING** 20–40 min.

Leader: The agenda has three parts. In the Gathering time you'll be getting to know each other through an "ice-breaker." This will be for your total group. The Study time has two parts: (1) Story and (2) Scripture. If you are short of time, skip the Story and move to the Scripture. Begin by reading out loud the Story or the Scripture to the whole group. Then divide into groups of 4 for the Study time. Finally, regather the total group for the Caring time. Keep to this agenda: (1) Gathering—10 minutes, (2) Study—30 minutes, and (3) Caring—20–40 minutes.

 **Songs of Home.** Use the questions below to get acquainted. Go around the group on the first question. Then go around on the next question.

1. Which of the following songs best describes your attitude toward your home when you were in high school?
   ❏ "House of Love" (Amy Grant)
   ❏ "Thank God, I'm a Country Boy" (John Denver)
   ❏ "We Gotta Get Out of This Place" (Beau Brummels)
   ❏ "Be It Ever So Humble ..." (Traditional)
   ❏ other:______________________________

2. If you were to sing a song about your childhood, what style of song would it most likely be?
   ❏ the blues—I've definitely paid my dues!
   ❏ hard rock—full of rebellion
   ❏ gospel—passionately religious
   ❏ folk music—simple and pure
   ❏ other:__________________

<table>
<tr><td>

SESSION

1

</td><td>

A Guiding Light
Epiphany of Our Lord - Matt. 2:1–12

</td></tr>
</table>

PURPOSE

To look at the light which God sends into our world today to guide us in our darkness.

FOR THE PASTOR

The following material you can use as input for your sermon preparation on this week's Gospel Scripture from the book of Matthew. For further input you may want to share and further comment on the story of Mother Teresa, which your study group(s) will be responding to during their session. Also, it's important to share in your sermon or homily your own response to the personal question (or other personally-oriented question) to model personal sharing for your congregation.

SCRIPTURE

2 **In the time of King Herod, after Jesus was born in Bethlehem of Judea, wise men from the East came to Jerusalem, 2asking, "Where is the child who has been born king of the Jews? For we observed his star at its rising, and have come to pay him homage." 3When King Herod heard this, he was frightened, and all Jerusalem with him; 4and calling together all the chief priests and scribes of the people, he inquired of them where the Messiah was to be born. 5They told him, "In Bethlehem of Judea; for so it has been written by the prophet:**

> **6"And you, Bethlehem, in the land of Judah,**
> **are by no means least among the rulers of Judah;**
> **for from you shall come a ruler**
> **who is to shepherd my people Israel.' "**

7Then Herod secretly called for the wise men and learned from them the exact time when the star had appeared. 8Then he sent them to Bethlehem, saying, "Go and search diligently for the child; and when you have found him, bring me word so that I may go and pay him homage." 9When they had heard the king, they set out; and there, ahead of them, went the star that they had seen at its rising, until it stopped over the place where the child was. 10When they saw that the star had stopped, they were overwhelmed with joy. 11On entering the house, they saw the child with Mary his mother; and they knelt down and paid him homage. Then, opening their treasure chests, they offered him gifts of gold, frankincense, and myrrh. 12And having been warned in a dream not to return to Herod, they left for their own country by another road.

Matthew 2:1–12

INTRODUCTION

Many people do not really know what "Epiphany" means. We're like the pirate "Smee" in the movie, *Hook*. When he gets an idea of how to get the best of Peter Pan, he says, "I think I just had an apostrophe," and Captain Hook says, "I think you mean an 'epiphany.' " Earlier Captain Hook had used the word, saying "all the jagged parts of my life have suddenly come together." That's something of the popular use of the word— a time when we have such a flash of insight that our life suddenly makes sense in a way it never had before. But an older use of the word is "an appearance or manifestation of a god or other supernatural being," and it is most often used to refer to the season commemorating the revealing of Jesus as the Christ to the Gentiles in the persons of the Magi (generally emphasized in the Western church) or the baptism of Jesus (generally emphasized in the Eastern church). These different definitions actually come together well because when Jesus revealed himself as God in our midst, he made it possible for many of us to "have all the jagged parts of our life come together" in a new, more meaningful way. A "new light" has shined in our lives, so that what was hidden in darkness and confusion now makes sense. The light which came from the Bethlehem star to guide the Magi is hence a type for the light which God always shines before us to show us the way.

<table>
<tr><td>NOTES ON
THE TEXT</td><td>

2:1 *King Herod.* Herod the Great was a shrewd but cruel monarch who was appointed by Rome to rule over Palestine. He reigned from 40 B.C. to 4 B.C. ***Bethlehem.*** Bethlehem was some 90 miles from Nazareth, a three- or four-day journey. Luke's Gospel tells us that the family had to go from Nazareth to Bethlehem for a census, possibly because that is where Joseph's clan originated, and he may have had property there. ***wise men.*** Also known as "Magi," these were astrologers who probably came from Babylon—modern Iran or Iraq.

2:2 *his star.* Attempts have been made to correlate the presence of this star with a variety of natural phenomena, including an unusual conjunction of Jupiter and Venus in 7 B.C., but little can be said with certainty. What is obvious, however, is that these astrologers saw in it a sign of a special messenger from God. Magi believed that a star could be a "fravashi" (a counterpart or angel) of a great person. ***at its rising.*** Some translations of this passage say "in the east." A rising star would be a good omen. It's significant that God used a foreign philosophy (astrology) to speak to non-Jewish people. It's significant also that while a Jewish king (Herod) would later plot to kill this new king, Gentile kings worship him, a parallel to how the Gentiles were later more receptive to the Gospel.

2:3 *he was frightened.* Toward the end of his reign Herod became paranoid that people were plotting to take over his throne. He actually had his favorite wife, her mother, two of her sons, and his oldest son murdered.

2:11 *the house.* Luke's narrative pictures Jesus' parents as temporary visitors to Bethlehem. In Matthew, it seems to be the place where they lived. Whatever the case, time has elapsed since Jesus' birth, since Jesus is no longer in a stable, but a house. He is also called a "child" (*paidion*) and not a "baby" (*brephos*). ***they knelt down and paid him***

</td></tr>
</table>

homage. The first people to worship Jesus in Matthew's account were Gentiles, hinting at the fact that Jesus had come not just for the Jews but for all nations. ***offered him gifts.*** Matthew no doubt thinks of Isaiah 60:6, where "those from Sheba," i.e. south Arabia, bring gold and incense. ***gold.*** Gold was the currency of kings. ***frankincense.*** It was a sweet-smelling gum that was burned during worship. ***myrrh.*** Myrrh was another gum, used as a perfume, as a medicine, and to embalm bodies. Taken together, the gifts could represent the identity of Jesus as the royal Son of God who gave his life for his people.

2:12 *a dream.* For the second time in this account, a dream plays a crucial role in the childhood of Jesus. The Magi are obedient to this vision and return home another way so as not to have to reveal to Herod the whereabouts of the child.

<table>
<tr><td>PERSONAL
QUESTION</td><td>Where were you born? What do you know about the circumstances surrounding your birth?</td></tr>
<tr><td>STORY</td><td>

The Calling of Mother Teresa. One of the best known persons of the modern church is Mother Teresa, who ministered to the poorest of the poor in Calcutta, India. Some think that to take on such a life, surrounded by poverty and death, would necessitate that someone be able to completely disregard their own happiness. But at least in the following story of when she wrestled with her call as an adolescent, Mother Teresa (born Agnes Bojaxhiu) was given a different understanding:

"She herself declared: 'I was still young, perhaps twelve years old, when in our family circle I said for the first time that I wanted to belong wholly to God. I thought this over for six years, and prayed about it. ...'

"She could still hear in her heart her mother's words: 'When you take on a task, do it willingly, otherwise do not accept it.' It was in this manner that the spiritual life she found in her family and then in the parish, and above all the example of her mother and of Fr. Jambrekovic, struck root at the soul of Agnes. She reflected and prayed a long time to come to know what path she should follow. For a time she even strove to free herself from these thoughts, and almost succeeded; but God would not leave her in peace. Before taking the final decision she asked for advice from all those around her in the family, from her mother above all, then from her sister and her friends. One evening (she tells us this herself) she went to her confessor and said to him: 'How can I know whether God is really calling me, and to what?' He told her: 'You can know by the happiness you feel. If you are glad at the thought that God may be calling you to serve him and your neighbor, this may well be the best proof of your vocation. A deep joy is like the compass which points out the projection for your life. One should follow this, even when one is venturing upon a difficult path.' "[1]

</td></tr>
</table>

[1] Lush Gjergji, *Mother Teresa: Her Life, Her Works* (Hyde Park, NY: New City Press, 1991), pp. 22–23.

Small Group
HANDOUT

WEEK 2: EPIPHANY 1
A Light From Heaven
Matthew 3:13–17

 **GATHERING**
10 min.

 **STUDY**
30 min.

 **CARING**
20–40 min.

Leader: The agenda has three parts. In the Gathering time you'll be getting to know each other through an "ice-breaker." This will be for your total group. The Study time has two parts: (1) Story and (2) Scripture. If you are short of time, skip the Story and move to the Scripture. Begin by reading out loud the Story or the Scripture to the whole group. Then divide into groups of 4 for the Study time. Finally, regather the total group for the Caring time. Keep to this agenda: (1) Gathering—10 minutes, (2) Study—30 minutes, and (3) Caring—20–40 minutes.

 **When I Was a Kid.** Go around on question 1 and let everyone share a page out of their life. Then go around again on question 2.

1. Develop a composite picture of your childhood home by completing the following statements (choose three):
   - The best thing about my family was ...
   - The best word to describe my mother was ...
   - The best word to describe my father was ...
   - The biggest tension in my family was ...
   - I think the biggest concern my parents had for me was ...
   - Probably the biggest sacrifice my parents made for me was ...

2. What aspects of your childhood home environment have you sought to recreate in your present home, and why?

<table>
<tr><td>

SESSION
2

</td><td>

A Light From Heaven
Epiphany 1 - Matthew 3:13–17

</td></tr>
</table>

PURPOSE

To consider how, in order to counter the darkness this world sometimes brings, we need a source of light beyond ourselves, from heaven.

FOR THE PASTOR

The following material you can use as input for your sermon preparation on this week's Gospel Scripture from the book of Matthew. For further input you may want to share and further comment on the story of St. Augustine, which your study group(s) will be responding to during their session. Also, it's important to share in your sermon or homily your own response to the personal question (or other personally-oriented question) to model personal sharing for your congregation.

SCRIPTURE

[13]Then Jesus came from Galilee to John at the Jordan, to be baptized by him. [14]John would have prevented him, saying, "I need to be baptized by you, and do you come to me?" [15]But Jesus answered him, "Let it be so now; for it is proper for us in this way to fulfill all righteousness." Then he consented. [16]And when Jesus had been baptized, just as he came up from the water, suddenly the heavens were opened to him and he saw the Spirit of God descending like a dove and alighting on him. [17]And a voice from heaven said, "This is my Son, the Beloved, with whom I am well pleased."

Matthew 3:13–17

INTRODUCTION

We all know that when things get confusing, heaven doesn't open up so a voice can talk to us—or at least we think we know that. It's never happened to us or anyone we have known personally, anyway. Many of us then hear of the story of the voice at Jesus' baptism with envy, wishing our own affirmation and direction from God could be so direct and obvious. But does that mean we don't get light from heaven? It's a matter of trust. Even those who witnessed the voice at Jesus' baptism would have had to trust their senses that what they heard was real. On our part we have to trust that the teachings that come to us through Scripture and the direction of the Holy Spirit are light from heaven for us as well. We sense that what it tells us "strikes home" and puts us in touch with God. Can we trust that sense?

3:13 *Then Jesus came.* Matthew 3:1–12 tells the story of John the Baptist, a prophet who called upon the Jews to repent and prepare themselves for the coming of the Lord. As a sign of repentance, he called upon people to be baptized. This was a radical demand since at the time only Gentiles who were converting to Judaism had to be baptized in order to wash away the "Gentile filth" with which they were associated. ***from Galilee to John at the Jordan.*** This was a journey of a few days. Galilee was a province to the north of where John was baptizing in the Jordan River in the province of Judea.

3:14 *... and do you come to me?* That Jesus was baptized was a confusing matter to the Christian community, since Jesus was proclaimed to be sinless and baptism is a symbol of repentance. Especially would it be embarrassing to John, if in fact he was himself aware of Jesus' divinity and sinless life, as it would make him all the more conscious of his own sin. But that is the way of God, that he uses sinners to perform his acts of grace!

3:15 *to fulfill all righteousness.* By being baptized Jesus showed by example what was expected of people who sought after righteousness.

3:16 *like a dove.* Matthew uses the symbol of a dove to communicate the coming of the Holy Spirit. The dove was not a common symbol in first-century Israel. But perhaps it communicates the gentler, more peaceful side of the Holy Spirit's presence, in contrast to the more powerful, more disturbing images of wind and fire used in Acts.

When Jesus had his "coming out" to begin his ministry, he came out of Galilee. Where was the neighborhood where you grew up and what was it like?

Augustine's Baptism. Augustine was one of the great early thinkers and writers of the Christian church. His *Confessions* is considered by some to be the greatest spiritual autobiography of all time. In it he tells of what he later considered to be a "wicked, misspent" youth, and a long spiritual and intellectual struggle as he sought to decide between the Christianity of his mother and the other philosophical and religious options of the day. Finally, he came to the point of committing to the Christian faith. In the following segment from his *Confessions* (addressed to God) he tells of his baptism on Easter in A.D. 387:

"Alypius likewise resolved to be born again in you, in company with me, for he was now clothed with that humility which befits your sacraments. ... We also joined to ourselves the boy Adeodatus, born of me in the flesh out of my sin. Well had you made him: he was almost fifteen years old, and in power of mind he surpassed many grave and learned men. ... To me his power of mind was a source of awe. Who except you is the worker of such miracles?

"Quickly you took his life away from the earth, and now I remember him with a more peaceful mind, for I have no fear for anything in his childhood or youth, and none at all for him as a man. We joined him to us, of equal age in your grace, to be instructed in your discipline. We were baptized, and anxiety over our past life fled away from us. ... How greatly did I weep during hymns and canticles, keenly affected by your sweet-singing Church! Those voices flowed into my ears, and your truth was distilled into my heart, and from that truth holy emotions overflowed, and the tears ran down, and amid those tears all was well with me."[1]

[1] John K. Ryan, translator, *The Confessions of St. Augustine,* (New York: Doubleday, 1960), p. 214.

Small Group
HANDOUT

WEEK 3: EPIPHANY 2
Seeing the Light
John 1:29–42

 GATHERING
10 min.

 STUDY
30 min.

 CARING
20–40 min.

Leader: The agenda has three parts. In the Gathering time you'll be getting to know each other through an "ice-breaker." This will be for your total group. The Study time has two parts: (1) Story and (2) Scripture. If you are short of time, skip the Story and move to the Scripture. Begin by reading out loud the Story or the Scripture to the whole group. Then divide into groups of 4 for the Study time. Finally, regather the total group for the Caring time. Keep to this agenda: (1) Gathering—10 minutes, (2) Study—30 minutes, and (3) Caring—20–40 minutes.

 **Emotional "Nutrients."** Go around on question 1 and let everyone share a page out of their life. Then go around again on question 2.

1. If you were to choose four components of a "well-balanced diet" to nourish your emotional well-being ("religious" activities are not included!), what would they be?

   ❐ getting hugs from friends
   ❐ attention from the opposite sex
   ❐ watching sports on TV
   ❐ watching old movies
   ❐ playing with my grandchildren
   ❐ camping in the mountains
   ❐ listening to music
   ❐ having time alone
   ❐ jogging
   ❐ taking a walk
   ❐ professional success
   ❐ shopping
   ❐ reading romance novels
   ❐ traveling
   ❐ fishing
   ❐ laying on the beach
   ❐ talking on the phone
   ❐ other:_______________

2. Which of the above do you feel most "hungry" for right now?

<table>
<tr><td>SESSION

3</td><td><h1>Seeing the Light</h1>

Epiphany 2 - John 1:29–42</td></tr>
</table>

PURPOSE

To consider how seeing the light which God shines into our lives is a choice we make, and to learn to choose to see it.

FOR THE PASTOR

The following material you can use as input for your sermon preparation on this week's Gospel Scripture from the book of John. For further input you may want to share and further comment on the story of C.S. Lewis, which your study group(s) will be responding to during their session. Also, it's important to share in your sermon or homily your own response to the personal question (or other personally-oriented question) to model personal sharing for your congregation.

SCRIPTURE

29 The next day he saw Jesus coming toward him and declared, "Here is the Lamb of God who takes away the sin of the world! 30 This is he of whom I said, 'After me comes a man who ranks ahead of me because he was before me.' 31 I myself did not know him; but I came baptizing with water for this reason, that he might be revealed to Israel." 32 And John testified, "I saw the Spirit descending from heaven like a dove, and it remained on him. 33 I myself did not know him, but the one who sent me to baptize with water said to me, 'He on whom you see the Spirit descend and remain is the one who baptizes with the Holy Spirit.' 34 And I myself have seen and have testified that this is the Son of God."

35 The next day John again was standing with two of his disciples, 36 and as he watched Jesus walk by, he exclaimed, "Look, here is the Lamb of God!" 37 The two disciples heard him say this, and they followed Jesus. 38 When Jesus turned and saw them following, he said to them, "What are you looking for?" They said to him, "Rabbi" (which translated means Teacher), "where are you staying?" 39 He said to them, "Come and see." They came and saw where he was staying, and they remained with him that day. It was about four o'clock in the afternoon. 40 One of the two who heard John speak and followed him was Andrew, Simon Peter's brother. 41 He first found his brother Simon and said to him, "We have found the Messiah" (which is translated Anointed). 42 He brought Simon to Jesus, who looked at him and said, "You are Simon son of John. You are to be called Cephas" (which is translated Peter).

John 1:29–42

It's not enough for a new light to shine in our lives. We must decide what we are going to do about that light. We need to decide whether we will allow that light in to brighten the darkness within us. In the Nazi concentration camp at Dachau, it is said that some of the prisoners (who yearned so desperately for their freedom) had been held captive for so long that when they were eventually released, they walked out into the sunlight, blinked nervously and then silently walked back into the familiar darkness of the prisons, to which they had become accustomed. Because darkness is something we can become accustomed to, we have to choose whether or not to see the light God shines into our lives. Seeing it means we sometimes have to give up the comfortable and familiar. But it also means we have the opportunity to be free from the limitations of darkness. Which will we choose?

1:29 *Lamb of God who takes away the sin of the world.* This first title for Jesus occurs only here and in 1 Peter 1:19. It refers to the Passover ritual in which a lamb was killed so that the wrath of God would "pass over" the home of the family which sprinkled his blood on its doorposts (Exodus 12:1–23). Note also that Isaiah referred to the Suffering Servant, equated by Christians to the Messiah, as one "led like a lamb to the slaughter" as he "took up our infirmities" (Isaiah 53).

1:30 *he was before me.* John speaks of the preexistence of Jesus. This Jesus also claimed for himself when he asserted that he predates, not simply John, but the Old Testament patriarch Abraham who lived two thousand years before this time.

1:34 *Son of God.* This a royal title used in the Old Testament to refer to Israel's kings who were called God's "sons" in that they had the right and power, under God, to exercise authority over the people (see Psalm 2:1–8). The author applies this to Jesus, who by virtue of his preexistence and identity with God, is God's Son in a unique sense. Whereas Jesus most often refers to himself as "the Son of Man" here we find his other relational connection emphasized.

1:38 *What are you looking for?* Jesus is very direct in getting the disciples to say why they are following him. ***Rabbi ... where are you staying?*** The disciples avoid answering Jesus' question, perhaps because they weren't sure what they were looking for.

1:42 *Cephas.* The Aramaic name, Cephas, and the Greek name, Peter, both mean "rock." Although Peter often seemed unstable during Jesus' time with him, after the Ascension Peter became the chief spokesman for the apostles (Acts 2:14).

PERSONAL QUESTION

When Andrew found something exciting he shared it with his brother Simon. When you were in junior high and you ran across something exciting, who was the first person you wanted to share it with?

STORY

God Breaks Through To C.S. Lewis. C.S. Lewis became one of the most popular Christian writers of modern time, writing both books to aid the Christian understanding of adults (like *Mere Christianity* and *Screwtape Letters*), as well as allegorical books for children (*The Chronicles of Narnia*). But there was a time in his life when he considered himself an atheist. He prided himself in his intellectual acumen, and saw Christianity as anti-intellectual. But over a period of time, God began to shed light into the darkness of C.S. Lewis, and he began to see things in a different way. He told the story of a pivotal moment in this transition in his autobiographical book, *Surprised by Joy:*

"Then I read Chesterton's *Everlasting Man* and for the first time saw the whole Christian outline of history set out in a form that seemed to me to make sense. Somehow I contrived not to be too badly shaken. ... But ... I had not long finished *The Everlasting Man* when something far more alarming happened to me. Early in 1926 the hardest boiled of all atheists I ever knew sat in my room on the other side of the fire and remarked that the evidence for the historicity of the Gospels was surprisingly good. ... To understand the shattering impact of it, you would need to know the man (who has certainly never since shown any interest in Christianity). If he, the cynic of cynics, the toughest of the toughs, were not—as I still would have put it—'safe,' where could I turn? Was there no escape?

"The odd thing was that before God closed in on me, I was in fact offered what now appears a moment of wholly free choice. In a sense, I was going up Headington Hill on the top of a bus. Without words and (I think) almost without images, a fact about myself was somehow presented to me. I became aware that I was holding something at bay, or shutting something out. Or, if you like, that I was wearing some stiff clothing, like corsets, or even a suit of armor, as if I were a lobster. I felt myself being, there and then, given a free choice. I could open the door or keep it shut; I could unbuckle the armor or keep it on. ... I chose to open, to unbuckle, to loosen the rein. ... I felt as if I were a man of snow at long last beginning to melt. ..."[1]

WEEK 4: EPIPHANY 3
Witnessing to the Light
Matthew 4:12–23

 **GATHERING**
10 min.

 **STUDY**
30 min.

 **CARING**
20–40 min.

Leader: The agenda has three parts. In the Gathering time you'll be getting to know each other through an "ice-breaker." This will be for your total group. The Study time has two parts: (1) Story and (2) Scripture. If you are short of time, skip the Story and move to the Scripture. Begin by reading out loud the Story or the Scripture to the whole group. Then divide into groups of 4 for the Study time. Finally, regather the total group for the Caring time. Keep to this agenda: (1) Gathering—10 minutes, (2) Study—30 minutes, and (3) Caring—20–40 minutes.

 **If You're Looking for Me ...** Go around on question #1, letting everyone share their answer, and then do the same with question #2.

1. Choose five of the following pairs and tell which option of the pair says best where you are most likely to be found.

   at McDonald's ___________________________________ at Chez Pierre's

   at K-Mart ___________________________________ at Saks Fifth Avenue

   at a ballgame ___________________________________ at a concert

   at a friends having coffee ___________________________________ at work, making deals

   seeking sand and surf ___________________________________ surfing the Internet

   finding new places ___________________________________ returning to old places

   at a children's program ___________________________________ at a board meeting

   tending livestock ___________________________________ in the stock market

2. If you are wanting not to be found, where do you go?

<table>
<tr><td>

SESSION

4
</td><td>

Witnessing to the Light
Epiphany 3 - Matthew 4:12–23
</td></tr>
</table>

PURPOSE

To learn how we can go beyond seeing the light to witnessing about that light to others.

FOR THE PASTOR

The following material you can use as input for your sermon preparation on this week's Gospel Scripture from the book of Matthew. For further input you may want to share and further comment on the story of Corrie ten Boom, which your study group(s) will be responding to during their session. Also, it's important to share in your sermon or homily your own response to the personal question (or other personally-oriented question) to model personal sharing for your congregation.

SCRIPTURE

[12]Now when Jesus heard that John had been arrested, he withdrew to Galilee. [13]He left Nazareth and made his home in Capernaum by the sea, in the territory of Zebulon and Naphtali, [14]so that what had been spoken through the prophet Isaiah might be fulfilled:

> *[15]Land of Zebulun, land of Naphtali,*
>> *on the road by the sea, across the Jordan,*
>>> *Galilee of the Gentiles—*
> *[16]the people who sat in darkness*
>> *have seen a great light,*
> *and for those who sat in the region and shadow of death*
>> *light has dawned."*

[17]From that time Jesus began to proclaim, "Repent, for the kingdom of heaven has come near."

[18]As he walked by the Sea of Galilee, he saw two brothers, Simon, who is called Peter, and Andrew his brother, casting a net into the sea—for they were fishermen. [19]And he said to them, "Follow me, and I will make you fish for people." [20]Immediately they left their nets and followed him. [21]As he went from there, he saw two other brothers, James son of Zebedee and his brother John, in the boat with their father Zebedee, mending their nets, and he called them. [22]Immediately they left the boat and their father, and followed him.

[23]Jesus went throughout Galilee, teaching in their synagogues and proclaiming the good news of the kingdom and curing every disease and every sickness among the people.

Matthew 4:12–23

Recent famous trials, like the O.J. Simpson case, have made some witnesses famous. People who were in a strategic place at a strategic time can witness to what happened in such a case, and can turn the case around. Not all of us can be that kind of a witness. But we have all witnessed some things; and if what we witness is exciting and life-changing, then shouldn't we tell others? Scripture tells us that light has come to a darkened world, and if we have ourselves seen that light—not just heard about it from a Sunday school teacher somewhere, but have really experienced it—then we are an "expert witness" and should tell our story. That is what this week's Scripture is about.

4:12 *Galilee* This was the northern province of Palestine. It was small, about 25 by 35 miles in size, but quite densely populated. At the time of Jesus approximately 350,000 people lived here, 100,000 of whom were Jews.

4:13 *Nazareth.* This was a village located in the hill country of Galilee 20 miles southwest of Capernaum. ***Capernaum.*** This was a town on the north end of the Sea of Galilee, three miles west of the River Jordan. It was the center of the fishing industry and the site of a custom's post. ***the territory of Zebulun and Naphtali.*** Israel was originally made up of 12 tribes descended from Jacob, and this was the region originally assigned to these two tribes. It was through this area that Assyria first marched when it defeated Israel, and carried most of her people into exile, but now they would be the first to see the light of Jesus Christ.

4:14–16 The coming of Jesus to this region fulfills the promise found in Isaiah 9:1–2. In its Old Testament setting, this prophecy promises the restoration of the land (which had been destroyed by the Assyrians) by a messianic king.

4:20 *Immediately they left.* According to 4:12–17 Jesus had been living and preaching in Capernaum. These fishermen probably had the chance to hear his message prior to their call. Still, what they did was an act of great faith and courage. In the first century you lived where you were born, you stayed in your family cluster and you took up your father's occupation.

This passage tells us that Jesus left his former home of Nazareth and made his home in Capernaum. Before that he and his family had lived for a while in Bethlehem, where he was born. What places have you called "home" in your life? Which was your favorite?

A Light Penetrates Prison. Corrie ten Boom and other members of her family were arrested for hiding Jews from the Nazis in Holland during World War II. Corrie went through many nightmarish experiences in concentration camps. But in the midst of it all, she also had many opportunities to witness to the light of Jesus Christ. In one instance she tells about, she had told a Nazi lieutenant about a ministry she had done with developmentally disabled people in Holland. After he disparaged work with such people as "a waste," she was bold to proclaim that in God's eyes such a person was of equal value to a Nazi Lieutenant. This caused him to dismiss her quickly, and made her think she had hurt her own cause. But the next morning she had a surprise. She tells of it in her book, *The Hiding Place:*

"And yet the following morning it was Lieutenant Rahms himself who unlocked my cell door and escorted me to the hearing. ... Gratefully I followed him to the farthest corner of the little yard where the air was still and warm. We settled our backs against the wall. 'I could not sleep last night,' the lieutenant said, 'thinking about that Book where you have read such different ideas. What else does it say in there?'

"On my closed eyelids the sun glimmered and blazed. 'It says,' I began slowly, 'that a Light has come into this world, so that we need no longer walk in the dark. Is there darkness in your life, Lieutenant?'

"There was a very long silence.

" 'There is a great darkness,' he said at last. 'I cannot bear the work I do here.'

"Then all at once he was telling me about his wife and children in Bremen, about their garden, their dogs, their summer hiking vacations. 'Bremen was bombed again last week. Each morning I ask myself, are they still alive?'

" 'There is One Who has them always in His sight, Lieutenant Rahms. Jesus is the Light the Bible shows to me, the Light that can shine even in such darkness as yours.'

"The man pulled the visor of his hat lower over his eyes; the skull-and-crossbones blinked in the sunlight. When he spoke it was so low I could hardly hear. 'What can you know of darkness like mine?' "[1]

[1] Corrie ten Boom, *The Hiding Place* (Minneapolis, MN: Worldwide Publications, 1971), pp. 166–167.

Small Group
HANDOUT

WEEK 5: EPIPHANY 4
A Light for the Lowly
Matthew 5:1–12

 **GATHERING**
10 min.

 **STUDY**
30 min.

 **CARING**
20–40 min.

Leader: The agenda has three parts. In the Gathering time you'll be getting to know each other through an "ice-breaker." This will be for your total group. The Study time has two parts: (1) Story and (2) Scripture. If you are short of time, skip the Story and move to the Scripture. Begin by reading out loud the Story or the Scripture to the whole group. Then divide into groups of 4 for the Study time. Finally, regather the total group for the Caring time. Keep to this agenda: (1) Gathering—10 minutes, (2) Study—30 minutes, and (3) Caring—20–40 minutes.

 **Music in My Life.** Put an **"X"** on each of the lines below—somewhere between the two extremes—to indicate how you are feeling right now about each area of your life. If time is limited, choose only two or three:

In my emotional life, I'm feeling like ...
"Blues in the Night" ____ **"Celebrate"**

In my family life, I'm feeling like ...
"Stormy Weather" ________________________________ **"The Sound of Music"**

In my spiritual life, I'm feeling like ...
"Sounds of Silence" ______________________________ **"Hallelujah Chorus"**

In my close relationships, I'm feeling like ...
"Love is a Battlefield" ______________________________ **"You Light Up My Life"**

As I look at my immediate future, I'm feeling like ...
"Yesterday" ________________________________ **"To Dream the Impossible Dream"**

<table>
<tr><td>SESSION

5</td><td><h1>A Light for the Lowly</h1>
Epiphany 4 - Matthew 5:1–12</td></tr>
</table>

PURPOSE

To understand how the light which God sent into the world has special importance for the lowly, the ones whom the world has forgotten or abused.

FOR THE PASTOR

The following material you can use as input for your sermon preparation on this week's Gospel Scripture from the book of Matthew. For further input you may want to share and further comment on the story of Mother Teresa, which your study group(s) will be responding to during their session. Also, it's important to share in your sermon or homily your own response to the personal question (or other personally-oriented question) to model personal sharing for your congregation.

SCRIPTURE

5 *When Jesus saw the crowds, he went up the mountain; and after he sat down, his disciples came to him. [2]Then he began to speak, and taught them, saying:*

[3]"Blessed are the poor in spirit, for theirs is the kingdom of heaven.

[4]"Blessed are those who mourn, for they will be comforted.

[5]"Blessed are the meek, for they will inherit the earth.

[6]"Blessed are those who hunger and thirst for righteousness, for they will be filled.

[7]"Blessed are the merciful, for they will receive mercy.

[8]"Blessed are the pure in heart, for they will see God.

[9]"Blessed are the peacemakers, for they will be called children of God.

[10]"Blessed are those who are persecuted for righteousness' sake, for theirs is the kingdom of heaven.

[11]"Blessed are you when people revile you and persecute you and utter all kinds of evil against you falsely on my account. [12]Rejoice and be glad, for your reward is great in heaven, for in the same way they persecuted the prophets who were before you."

Matthew 5:1–12

INTRODUCTION

Of all the people in the world who need a light, it is those who are down who need it the most, and are most looking for it. When the world has rejected you, when success as the world defines it has eluded you, when you are left alone in one of the dark and empty corners of life, finding a new light becomes your only hope. Some despair of ever finding such a light. Thus we have the old joke, "There's a light at the end of the tunnel—but I think it's a train coming from the other way!" But the Good

News of Jesus Christ is that "The light shines in the darkness, and the darkness did not overcome it" (John 1:5).

5:1–2 *the mountain.* To the original Jewish readers, this would have been an inescapable allusion to when Moses delivered the Law to Israel from Mt. Sinai (see Deut. 18:15). ***sat down.*** When rabbis taught they would sit rather than stand. This accents Jesus' authoritative position.

5:3–10 The "Beatitudes" are so named because in the Latin Bible each of the eight statements began with the word "beatus." Such pronouncements of blessedness were particularly common in the Psalms.

5:3 *poor in spirit.* This phrase does not refer to those who are poor in the material sense, but to those who acknowledge their need for God. These are the people who are humble of spirit.

5:4 *those who mourn.* This does not refer to the bereaved in general but to those who mourn over their own sin, the loss they experience as a result of following God, and over the pain that evil in general brings to the whole world.

5:5 *the meek.* This involves a lifestyle marked by gentleness, humility and courteousness.

5:6 *hunger and thirst for righteousness.* As hungry and thirsty people devote their entire energy to finding food and water so those in the kingdom feel a deep-seated, intense longing for pursuing God's way.

5:8 *pure in heart.* The call is for a single-minded pursuit of God's way with every facet of our being. ***see God.*** In the Old Testament this term described what it meant to experience God's favor.

5:12 *reward is great in heaven.* "Heaven" is the way Matthew refers to God. The point is not that their reward will only be after death, but rather that it will be experienced in the presence of God. Here we might also note that the reward paired with each of these Beatitudes is not limited to that Beatitude, but rather the implication is that people who do these things will receive all these rewards.

When in your life have you most felt like an outcast leper?

God's Love for Lepers. There is perhaps no person in modern times who has become more respected and loved for their work with wounded and dying souls than Mother Teresa. One group she particularly worked with was the lepers in India. These are indeed a lowly people. Mother Teresa talks about them in her biography by Lush Gjergji, *Mother Teresa: Her Life, Her Works:*

"It is very difficult to convince people in India that God never condemned people to suffer. We know of cases of stark tragedy in which people cured of leprosy were slain, sometimes by members of their own families. For this reason we resolved to build little villages for them, where they could live, work and eventually have a family. Today leprosy can be treated successfully; obviously if it is caught in time. It takes about six months. Thanks to our benefactors the work is proceeding well, and many people have recovered the will to live. ...

"There are thousands and millions of lepers in the world. One Christmas I went to visit them, and told them that God loved them very specially; that all they had was God's gift; that God was close to them; that their illness was no sin. An old man, hardly able to move, with difficulty came up to me and said: 'Please, repeat that once more; I never before heard anything of the kind. All my life I only heard that nobody wanted me. How beautiful it is to know that God loves me!' "[1]

[1]Lush Gjergji, *Mother Teresa: Her Life, Her Works* (Hyde Park, NY: New City Press, 1991), pp. 64–65.

Small Group
HANDOUT

WEEK 6: EPIPHANY 5

The Light in Us
Matthew 5:13–20

 **GATHERING**
10 min.

 **STUDY**
30 min.

 **CARING**
20–40 min.

Leader: The agenda has three parts. In the Gathering time you'll be getting to know each other through an "ice-breaker." This will be for your total group. The Study time has two parts: (1) Story and (2) Scripture. If you are short of time, skip the Story and move to the Scripture. Begin by reading out loud the Story or the Scripture to the whole group. Then divide into groups of 4 for the Study time. Finally, regather the total group for the Caring time. Keep to this agenda: (1) Gathering—10 minutes, (2) Study—30 minutes, and (3) Caring—20–40 minutes.

 **Myself as a Work of Art.** If you were a famous work of art, which of the following would you like to be? Choose one and share it with your group.

MONA LISA—so I could spread my smile to everyone who needs one

THE THINKER—to inspire people to go beyond the superficial

MOUNT RUSHMORE—so I could inspire people to patriotism

MICHELANGELO'S DAVID—the essence of health and masculinity

VENUS DE MILO—the essence of health and feminity

SISTINE CHAPEL CEILING—so I could inspire everyone to look up

STATUE OF LIBERTY—so I could eternally inspire the downtrodden

AMERICAN GOTHIC—to remind people of good, solid country values

The Light in Us
Epiphany 5 - Matthew 5:13–20

PURPOSE

To recognize that God has put a light within us, the light of his presence and love, that is meant to be shared with others.

FOR THE PASTOR

The following material you can use as input for your sermon preparation on this week's Gospel Scripture from the book of Matthew. For further input you may want to share and further comment on the story of Albert Schweitzer, which your study group(s) will be responding to during their session. Also, it's important to share in your sermon or homily your own response to the personal question (or other personally-oriented question) to model personal sharing for your congregation.

SCRIPTURE

13"You are the salt of the earth; but if salt has lost its taste, how can its saltiness be restored? It is no longer good for anything, but is thrown out and trampled under foot.

14"You are the light of the world. A city built on a hill cannot be hid. 15No one after lighting a lamp puts it under the bushel basket, but on the lampstand, and it gives light to all in the house. 16In the same way, let your light shine before others, so that they may see your good works and give glory to your Father in heaven.

17"Do not think that I have come to abolish the law or the prophets; I have come not to abolish but to fulfill. 18For truly I tell you, until heaven and earth pass away, not one letter, not one stroke of a letter, will pass from the law until all is accomplished. 19Therefore, whoever breaks one of the least of these commandments, and teaches others to do the same, will be called least in the kingdom of heaven; but whoever does them and teaches them will be called great in the kingdom of heaven. 20For I tell you, unless your righteousness exceeds that of the scribes and Pharisees, you will never enter the kingdom of heaven.

Matthew 5:13–20

INTRODUCTION

A song that was popular a number of years ago declared, "You light up my life!" But whose life do we light up? That is in fact what we are called to do—light up the life of the people around us. Of course, we cannot do that on the basis of our own natural light. To try to do so would imply that our light is better than others, and it would deny the darkness inside of us that most of us are only all too aware is there. No, we must be like the moon, reflecting the greater Light that shines on us—the light not of the sun, but the Son. As Jesus sheds his loving light on our soul, and we feel the warmth and direction of that life, we must then share that light with others. Where we have been listened to, we must listen. Where we have been nurtured, we must nurture. Where Christ has sacrificed for us, we must also give ourselves up for others. If we are in Christ, there is a light in us, and we must share it.

5:13 *salt*. Salt was a basic commodity in the ancient world. It was used to season, preserve and purify food. In the days before refrigeration, meat could be preserved indefinitely if properly salted and cured. In like manner, the children of God are to flavor the world around them with God's ways to prevent it from going rancid. ***lost its taste*.** Pure salt does not lose its taste. However, what was popularly called "salt" was in fact a white powder which, while containing sodium chloride, also contained much else. Of this dust the sodium chloride was probably the most soluble component and so the most easily washed out. The residue of white powder looked like salt, but it neither tasted nor acted like salt.

5:14b–15 *the house*. Houses were typically simple one room structures. A candle or lamp lit in any part of such a house would obviously shed light throughout the whole structure. Some commentators wonder if Jesus was here contrasting the way he wanted the Christian community to be with the community of the Essenes who lived a monastic life separated from the normal life of Israel. Although they called themselves the "sons of light" they had effectively hidden that light from the rest of Israel. The Christian community was not to follow that lead, but to live out their distinctive character in the midst of the world. It is in so doing that the light can be seen.

5:17 *the law or the prophets*. The law was the way the Jews referred to the first five books of the Old Testament while the prophets refer to the major and minor prophets as well as the historical books like Kings and Chronicles. ***fulfill*.** By his teaching Jesus seeks to give full expression to the intention of the law. In contrast, by their preoccupation with the details of the law, the Pharisees and other religious leaders of the day, for all their concern about the law, often overlooked its true purpose.

5:18 *stroke of a letter*. Some Hebrew and Aramaic characters are distinguishable only by a small line or dot.

Tell of a time when you really felt you did "let your light shine"—a time you had a positive influence on someone, or made a difference with a community or world situation?

Albert Schweitzer's Happiness. Albert Schweitzer grew up as the son of a minister, and went on to become a minister himself. In addition, he was a renowned scholar and well-respected musician. But at the age of 30, he set all of that aside and decided to go into medical school for the express purpose of going to Africa and filling the need of the people there for medical care. In his autobiography, *Out of My Life and Thought,* he shared some of his thinking behind that decision:

"... It struck me as inconceivable that I should be allowed to lead such a happy life while I saw so many people around me struggling with sorrow and suffering. Even at school I had felt stirred whenever I caught a glimpse of the miserable home surroundings of some of my classmates and compared them with the ideal conditions in which we children of the parsonage at Gunsbach had lived. At the university, enjoying the good fortune of studying and even getting some results in scholarship and the arts, I could not help but think continually of others who were denied that good fortune by their material circumstances or their health.

"One brilliant summer morning at Gunsbach, during Whitsuntide holidays—it was in 1896—as I awoke, the thought came to me that I must not accept this good fortune as a matter of course, but must give something in return.

"While outside the birds sang I reflected on this thought, and before I had gotten up I came to the conclusion that until thirty I could consider myself justified in devoting myself to scholarship and the arts, but after that I would devote myself directly to serving humanity. I had already tried many times to find the meaning that lay hidden in the saying of Jesus: 'Whoever shall lose his life for My sake and the Gospels shall save it.' Now I had found the answer. I could now add outward to inward happiness."[1]

---

[1] Albert Schweitzer, *Out of My Life and Thought* (New York: Henry Holt & Co., 1949), p. 82.

Small Group
HANDOUT

WEEK 7: EPIPHANY 6
Living the Light
Matthew 5:21–37

 **GATHERING**
10 min.

 **STUDY**
30 min.

 **CARING**
20–40 min.

Leader: The agenda has three parts. In the Gathering time you'll be getting to know each other through an "ice-breaker." This will be for your total group. The Study time has two parts: (1) Story and (2) Scripture. If you are short of time, skip the Story and move to the Scripture. Begin by reading out loud the Story or the Scripture to the whole group. Then divide into groups of 4 for the Study time. Finally, regather the total group for the Caring time. Keep to this agenda: (1) Gathering—10 minutes, (2) Study—30 minutes, and (3) Caring—20–40 minutes.

 **The Light We Shine.** Over the past few weeks, we have gotten to know each other better. Knowing what you know now, what kind of light best describes each of the members in your group? For each of the lights below, choose a group member who best fits that category. Share these with each other in a spirit of affirmation.

CAMPFIRE LIGHT: You give warmth and light to the cold night.

FLASHLIGHT: You showed insight that brought light into an area that has been dark for me.

100-WATT BULB: Your personality lights up the room!

MOONLIGHT: You reflect well the light of the Son.

FIREPLACE LIGHT: You bring people together around your warmth and crackling flames.

SUNLIGHT: You are a natural light that gives life to those around you.

NEON LIGHT: You bring personality, flash and color to the group.

CANDLELIGHT: You help provide a relaxed, gentle mood.

<table>
<tr><td>

SESSION

7

</td><td>

Living the Light
Epiphany 6 - Matthew 5:21–37

</td></tr>
</table>

<table>
<tr><td>

PURPOSE

</td><td>

To look at what it means, in a practical way, to live the light that Jesus brought into the world.

</td></tr>
<tr><td>

FOR THE PASTOR

</td><td>

The following material you can use as input for your sermon preparation on this week's Gospel Scripture from the book of Matthew. For further input you may want to share and further comment on the story of St. Francis of Assisi, which your study group(s) will be responding to during their session. Also, it's important to share in your sermon or homily your own response to the personal question (or other personally-oriented question) to model personal sharing for your congregation.

</td></tr>
<tr><td>

SCRIPTURE

</td><td>

[21] "You have heard that it was said to those of ancient times, 'You shall not murder'; and 'whoever murders shall be liable to judgment.' [22] But I say to you that if you are angry with a brother or sister, you will be liable to judgment; and if you insult a brother or sister, you will be liable to the council; and if you say, 'You fool,' you will be liable to the hell of fire. [23] So when you are offering your gift at the altar, if you remember that your brother or sister has something against you, [24] leave your gift there before the altar and go; first be reconciled to your brother or sister, and then come and offer your gift. [25] Come to terms quickly with your accuser while you are on the way to court with him, or your accuser may hand you over to the judge, and the judge to the guard, and you will be thrown into prison. [26] Truly I tell you, you will never get out until you have paid the last penny.

[27] "You have heard that it was said, 'You shall not commit adultery.' [28] But I say to you that everyone who looks at a woman with lust has already committed adultery with her in his heart. [29] If your right eye causes you to sin, tear it out and throw it away; it is better for you to lose one of your members than for your whole body to be thrown into hell. [30] And if your right hand causes you to sin, cut it off and throw it away; it is better for you to lose one of your members than for your whole body to go into hell.

[31] "It was also said, 'Whoever divorces his wife, let him give her a certificate of divorce.' [32] But I say to you that anyone who divorces his wife, except on the ground of unchastity, causes her to commit adultery; and whoever marries a divorced woman commits adultery.

[33] "Again, you have heard that it was said to those of ancient times, 'You shall not swear falsely, but carry out the vows you have made to the Lord.' [34] But I say to you, Do not swear at all, either by heaven, for it is the throne of God, [35] or by the earth, for it is his footstool, or by Jerusalem, for it is the

</td></tr>
</table>

INTRODUCTION

An Associated Press story from a few years ago told of a janitor at a university that found some old pamphlets that had been eaten through by termites. The title of the pamphlets was ... "Control of Termites"! This reminds us that it does no good to have a light come into our world if we do not live according to that light. "Living the light" means more than the witnessing to others that we have talked about—it means letting that light so permeate all we are and all we do that it becomes an inseparable part of us. It shines forth whether we are alone with no one watching what we do, or whether we are in a crowd that opposes what we believe is right and good. It shines because that is the nature of light, to shine! It shines within, to enlighten our own darkness; and it shines without, to enlighten the darkness where we live. When our light shines in this way, Christ's work is completed in us.

NOTES ON THE TEXT

5:21–22 The Law says "do not murder" (Exodus 20:13) but Jesus focuses on that which gives rise to murder. **angry.** The Greek word used here describes deep-seated, smoldering, inner anger, rather than a flash of anger. **council.** This refers to the Sanhedrin, a group of 70 Jewish men who were the official ruling body of the Jews. **hell.** Literally, *Gehenna*, a ravine outside Jerusalem where children were once sacrificed to the god Molech (1 Kings 11:7). Jews considered it a defiled place, good only as a garbage dump which was continually burning. Gehenna became a symbol for the place of punishment and spiritual death.

5:27–28 with lust. Just as anger is at the root of murder, so too lust is the root of adultery. Jesus' intention is not to prohibit a natural sexual attraction, but the deliberate harboring of desire for an illicit relationship.

5:29–30 Jesus is speaking in hyperbole, using overstatement and dramatic imagery in order to make his point about the importance of inward purity. **right eye / hand.** The right eye or hand would be considered to be the one that a person could least afford to do without. Jesus is driving home the point that entering the kingdom is so important one ought to be willing to make any sacrifice to get there. Of course, if we took this literally, most, if not all, of us would be without our right eye and right hand!

5:31–32 divorce. Although in Jesus' day Deuteronomy 24:1–4 was used to sanction divorce, its original intent was not to justify divorce but simply to establish a procedure to protect women from capricious treatment by husbands who alone had the right of divorce. Jesus' words were not to lay an extra burden on unhappy couples, but to take a burden off of oppressed women. The application of this teaching is much debated today. What is clear is that marriage is intended to be lifelong, and that anything short of that is failure. While laws making allowance for human weakness, like the Deuteronomy passage, may exist, they do not mean divorce is something that is to be treated as an acceptable part of life.

5:34 *Do not swear at all.* Jesus goes beyond the Old Testament by pointing out the problem behind the fact that a person resorts to oath-taking in order to be trusted. Contrary to what some rabbis taught, according to Jesus it does not matter whether you swear upon God's name or anything else: a person's word alone should be sufficient to guarantee the accuracy of a statement. The issue in this statement is not so much oath-taking (Jesus took an oath in 26:62–64) as it is speaking the truth.

PERSONAL
QUESTION

When you were a child in grade school, what derogatory name(s) do you remember the other children calling you? How did you react?

STORY

St. Francis Builds a Church. Francis of Assisi grew up as the son of a wealthy merchant, and was known more for partying and spending money than for any spiritual pursuits. But when he was converted he turned away from worldly wealth, and took on the garb of the poor. He also had a vision in a small, broken-down church at San Damiano, that God wanted him to personally take on the rebuilding of that church. His biographer, Julien Green, tells the story:

"Francis didn't forget the poor church that the Lord, as he thought, had told him to repair; so, ... he went back to San Damiano to begin work there. But the purse full of golden coins was no longer on the window ledge, and building materials cost money. That was a problem, but not for him. With a simplicity that still amazes us, Francis followed the evangelical counsel to the letter and, trusting God's promise, he asked so as to receive. But how does one go about begging for stones?

"He began going up and down the streets of Assisi, crying out, 'Whoever gives me a stone will get a reward from the Lord. Whoever gives me two will get two rewards. Whoever gives me three, will get three rewards.' The first response was stunned surprise. So, to start things rolling, he sang of God with that charming voice known to everyone in town. There may have been some smiles and some snide remarks, but the unexpected question and the sweet, joyful melody finally took effect; and the stones appeared, one here, another there. A short while ago they were throwing stones to insult and hurt him ... and now they were bringing them to him like presents. Big ones and little ones, he accepted everything, returning to San Damiano with his harvest of rocks on his shoulders, exhausted but happy. ...

"The rougher work of repairing crumbling walls was still to be done, but here Francis showed he was an old hand, having been well trained by the people of Assisi when he helped build the town walls after the fortress had been demolished. ... And as he sang then in exultation of victory, he sang now of the joy of obeying what he thought was the Savior's wish."[1]

---

[1]Julien Green, *God's Fool: The Life and Times of Francis of Assisi* (San Francisco: Harper & Row, 1983), pp. 86–87.

SERENDIPITY

Small Group
HANDOUT

WEEK 8: EPIPHANY 7
A Light of Love
Matthew 5:38–48

 GATHERING
10 min.

 STUDY
30 min.

 CARING
20–40 min.

Leader: The agenda has three parts. In the Gathering time you'll be getting to know each other through an "ice-breaker." This will be for your total group. The Study time has two parts: (1) Story and (2) Scripture. If you are short of time, skip the Story and move to the Scripture. Begin by reading out loud the Story or the Scripture to the whole group. Then divide into groups of 4 for the Study time. Finally, regather the total group for the Caring time. Keep to this agenda: (1) Gathering—10 minutes, (2) Study—30 minutes, and (3) Caring—20–40 minutes.

 **Life Is a Beach.** A popular bumper sticker said, "LIFE IS A BEACH!" Is it? What has life been for you? Choose from one of the following or make up your own:

"LIFE IS A BEACH!"

"LIFE WAS A BEACH"—until the tidal wave hit!

"LIFE IS A MOUNTAIN"—full of challenging ascents and beautiful vistas

"LIFE IS A WINDING RIVER"—continually changing, with a new view around every corner

"LIFE IS A DESERT"—a hostile place where you fight for what you get

"LIFE IS A DESERT MIRAGE"—You never know what is real.

"LIFE IS A FARMER'S FIELD"—What you get depends on what you put into it.

"LIFE IS A TOXIC-WASTE DUMP"—We're killing each other!

other:____

<table>
<tr><td>SESSION

8</td><td><h1>A Light of Love</h1>
Epiphany 7 - Matthew 5:38–48</td></tr>
</table>

PURPOSE

To show how love is the greatest light we can shine into our own life or the life of another.

FOR THE PASTOR

The following material you can use as input for your sermon preparation on this week's Gospel Scripture from the book of Matthew. For further input you may want to share and further comment on the story of Desmond Tutu, which your study group(s) will be responding to during their session. Also, it's important to share in your sermon or homily your own response to the personal question (or other personally-oriented question) to model personal sharing for your congregation.

SCRIPTURE

[38]*"You have heard that it was said, 'An eye for an eye and a tooth for a tooth.'* [39]*But I say to you, Do not resist an evildoer. But if anyone strikes you on the right cheek, turn the other also;* [40]*and if anyone wants to sue you and take your coat, give your cloak as well;* [41]*and if anyone forces you to go one mile, go also the second mile.* [42]*Give to everyone who begs from you, and do not refuse anyone who wants to borrow from you.*

[43]*"You have heard that it was said, 'You shall love your neighbor and hate your enemy.'* [44]*But I say to you, Love your enemies and pray for those who persecute you,* [45]*so that you may be children of your Father in heaven; for he makes his sun rise on the evil and on the good, and sends rain on the righteous and on the unrighteous.* [46]*For if you love those who love you, what reward do you have? Do not even the tax collectors do the same?* [47]*And if you greet only your brothers and sisters, what more are you doing than others? Do not even the Gentiles do the same?* [48]*Be perfect, therefore, as your heavenly Father is perfect."*

Matthew 5:38–48

INTRODUCTION

Many of us are becoming more and more aware of the ugly and evil acts that are done in this world—child abuse, racial hatred, drive-by shootings, pushing drugs to children, and more. But what we don't know is what to do about it. Certainly, evil is a complex problem and we should not think too simplistically when searching for solutions. But great evil was also a part of Christ's world, too. A king slaughtered infants and toddlers in Bethlehem shortly after he was born. Many roads were not safe to travel alone. Christ was crucified because of gross injustice in the court system. And in the midst of such acts, what did Christ say?—Love your enemies! The more evil abounds, the more we must love to counter the effects of that evil. Many would like a simpler, less demanding solution—spend more dollars on prisons, hire more police, and it will be solved. Such actions may be necessary, but they will not solve the problem because they do not get at the root. The root is that evil is a contagion that spreads when we meet evil with evil. Love is the only effective prescription. Jesus knew that. Jesus lived that. Can we?

5:38 *An eye for an eye ...* This is said to be the oldest law in the world, found in non-Jewish as well as Jewish culture (Ex. 21:23–24; Lev. 24:20; Deut. 19:21). The law's original intent was not to require "eye for eye and tooth for tooth," but to establish the principle of limited, reciprocal punishment for crimes. It was to limit the practice where persons and tribes would resort to an ever-escalating style of revenge for harm done by another person or tribe.

5:39 *Do not resist an evildoer.* Jesus totally rejects the thought of personal revenge. This does not mean one shouldn't fight evil, since who did that better than Jesus himself? What it does mean is that we should resist using the weapons of evil—violence and retaliation. ***strikes you on the right cheek.*** This is the first of three examples of non-retaliation. What is in view here is not so much an act of physical assault, but a gesture of contempt that would normally provoke a hostile response.

5:40 *coat.* The close-fitting undergarment made out of cotton or linen and having sleeves. ***cloak.*** The outer robe which was more valuable than the coat that was demanded. The poor often used this as a coverlet at night. For this reason the law prohibited seizing a person's cloak as the payment of a debt (Ex. 22:25–6).

5:41 *forces you to go one mile.* The Greek word translated forces originally had to do with the Persian royal mail. Couriers could make people carry the king's messages. Here the word refers to any kind of forced labor. The Roman mile was a little shorter than the English mile.

5:42 *Give to everyone.* The aim is not to encourage lending to irresponsible people, but to encourage a free spirit of generosity as opposed to a narrow assessment of personal gain.

5:43 *hate your enemy.* The Jewish law never commanded the Jew to hate his or her enemy. However, there are many passages in the Old Testament that permit and even encourage hostility and retaliation (see for instance, Psalm17:8–14; 18: 37– 42).

5:44 *Love your enemies.* The word used for "love" here is "agape." This is love that shows itself not by what a person feels, but by what that person does. Agape love is benevolent action done on the behalf of another without the expectation of reward.

5:46 *tax collectors.* Tax collectors grew rich by charging people more than what was required (only they knew what was required by Rome), keeping the excess for themselves. A tax collector was, therefore, considered to be a traitor to Israel.

5:48 *Be perfect.* The Greek word used for "perfect" is *teleois,* which means "having attained the end or purpose." A thing is perfect if it fulfills the purpose for which it was made. In the creation account in the Old Testament, the purpose of men and women is stated: "Then God said, 'Let us make humankind in our image, according to our likeness ... .' " (Gen. 1:26). Thus men and women are "perfect" when they live out God's ways and so demonstrate that they are made in God's image. According to Sherman E. Johnson, "When Jesus says that his followers must be perfect, he probably does not expect that they will be absolutely flawless. 'Straight' or 'square' would be more accurate. ..."[1]

<table><tr><td>

PERSONAL QUESTION

</td><td>

When you were a child in grade school, who was the child who bullied you or gave you the hardest time? What kind of things did this person do to you?

</td></tr><tr><td>

STORY

</td><td>

Desmond Tutu's Struggle to Love. Desmond Tutu has been at the forefront of the fight against the apartheid that cursed his country for so long. The battle was of course partly personal because he himself had been a victim of that apartheid his entire life. An important part of his battle was the struggle to forgive his white oppressors. That became particularly difficult after he and his family went to England for a while and experienced what it was like to live in a less oppressive social system. His biographer, Shirley DuBoulay, writes of his experience in *Tutu: Voice of the Voiceless:*

</td></tr></table>

"It was indeed hard for the Tutus once again to become second-class citizens. They had known what to expect, but found that no preparation could reconcile them to their racially divided country. Soon after they returned to South Africa Desmond wrote to Martin Kenyon:

> " 'I don't want to sound melodramatic, but it is extremely difficult being back here, having to ask permission from various white officials to visit my parents! Having to carry my heavy passbook and look out for entrances meant especially for us ... . It is as well that Our Lord expects us not to like but to love our enemies and neighbors. It will be extremely difficult to love the white man as it is. Awful sentiment isn't it?'

"It is easy to take Desmond's lack of bitterness for granted, to forget that it is something for which he has had to struggle, that he prays constantly for the strength to win this struggle, even pleading for help from friends. He wrote, again to Martin Kenyon, 'Pray for us that we may not succumb to the temptation to hate and become bitter.' "[2]

[1] From *The Interpreter's Bible,* ed. George Buttrick Vol. 7: New Testament Articles—Matthew and Mark (Nashville: Abingdon Press, 1951), pp.304–305.

[2] Shirley DuBoulay, *Tutu: Voice of the Voiceless* (London, England: Hodder & Stoughton Publishers, 1988), p. 69.

Small Group
HANDOUT

WEEK 9: EPIPHANY 8
A Light on Our Priorities
Matthew 6:24–34

 **GATHERING**
10 min.

 **STUDY**
30 min.

 **CARING**
20–40 min.

Leader: The agenda has three parts. In the Gathering time you'll be getting to know each other through an "ice-breaker." This will be for your total group. The Study time has two parts: (1) Story and (2) Scripture. If you are short of time, skip the Story and move to the Scripture. Begin by reading out loud the Story or the Scripture to the whole group. Then divide into groups of 4 for the Study time. Finally, regather the total group for the Caring time. Keep to this agenda: (1) Gathering—10 minutes, (2) Study—30 minutes, and (3) Caring—20–40 minutes.

 **Desert Island.** If you were stranded on a desert island, which of the following persons (excluding family) would you like to be stranded with and why?

❏ Bill Nye, the Science Guy	❏ Cindy Crawford
❏ Tom Cruise	❏ Gilligan
❏ Mother Teresa	❏ Robin Williams
❏ Arnold Schwarzenegger	❏ Julia Roberts
❏ Colin Powell	❏ Bill Gates
❏ Bob Vila	❏ Whitney Houston
❏ Robert Schuller	❏ Dr. C. Everett Koop

<table>
<tr><td>SESSION
9</td><td># A Light on Our Priorities
Epiphany 8 - Matthew 6:24–34</td></tr>
</table>

PURPOSE

To examine the light that Jesus has shed on what our priorities are and what they should be.

FOR THE PASTOR

The following material you can use as input for your sermon preparation on this week's Gospel Scripture from the book of Matthew. For further input you may want to share and further comment on the story of Thomas Merton, which your study group(s) will be responding to during their session. Also, it's important to share in your sermon or homily your own response to the personal question (or other personally-oriented question) to model personal sharing for your congregation

SCRIPTURE

[24]**"No one can serve two masters; for a slave will either hate the one and love the other, or be devoted to the one and despise the other. You cannot serve God and wealth.**

[25]**"Therefore I tell you, do not worry about your life, what you will eat or what you will drink, or about your body, what you will wear. Is not life more than food, and the body more than clothing?** [26]**Look at the birds of the air; they neither sow nor reap nor gather into barns, and yet your heavenly Father feeds them. Are you not of more value than they?** [27]**And can any of you by worrying add a single hour to your span of life?** [28]**And why do you worry about clothing? Consider the lilies of the field, how they grow; they neither toil nor spin,** [29]**yet I tell you, even Solomon in all his glory was not clothed like one of these.** [30]**But if God so clothes the grass of the field, which is alive today and tomorrow is thrown into the oven, will he not much more clothe you—you of little faith?** [31]**Therefore do not worry, saying, 'What will we eat?' or 'What will we drink?' or 'What will we wear?'** [32]**For it is the Gentiles who strive for all these things; and indeed your heavenly Father knows that you need all these things.** [33]**But strive first for the kingdom of God and his righteousness, and all these things will be given to you as well.**

[34]**"So do not worry about tomorrow, for tomorrow will bring worries of its own. Today's trouble is enough for today.**

Matthew 6:24–34

"Don't Worry; Be Happy!" Thus declared a song by Bobby McFarren just a few years ago. The simple song became very popular, largely because the message of the song struck home with millions of stressed Americans. Jesus taught the same thing, and he told people that the key to being able to avoid worry was to trust God and keep your priorities straight. If we focus on material acquisition, then we will as a matter of course worry, because we are focusing life on things that are transient. But if we focus on the kingdom of God and trust God for our material needs, then we are investing our life in that which is permanent, and we need not worry about it one day being gone. Of course, trusting God for our material needs is easier said than done, but Jesus went on to live out his own teaching. He relied on God's people for his provision, and when his very life was threatened, he kept his "eyes on the prize" and acted in obedience to his heavenly Father. In a world where there is so much to distract us, his example, as well as his words, is vital.

6:25 *do not worry*. This is a more accurate phrase than the "take no thought for" of the old King James Version. We are not counseled against thinking about and planning for the future: we are counseled against letting worrying about the future incapacitate us so we cannot properly serve God.

6:27 *add a single hour*. Other versions, like the King James Version, read "add one cubit to your height," which most people would desire less than adding to their lifespan (a cubit is the length of a forearm, about 18 inches). In either case, the point is the same—worry accomplishes nothing practical.

6:28 *the lilies of the field*. These flowers cannot be identified with certainty, since the word is used of all kinds of wild flowers, but some think what was being referred to were scarlet anemones.

6:29 *Solomon*. Solomon, the third king of Israel, was noted for his fabulous wealth (1 Kings 10:14–29).

6:30 *thrown into the oven*. Dry flowers and grass were used to fuel the ovens in which people baked their bread.

6:32 *and indeed your heavenly Father knows*. Jesus does not deny that food, drink and clothing are important things. He is just saying that once we learn to trust God's provision, these are no longer the priorities our life is focused on.

6:34 *Today's trouble is enough for today*. We note the Christian does encounter troubles. God does not automatically take these away. But what is counseled is to take things "one day at a time" and trust God's provision. When we do, we can handle it!

What were the "big worries" you remember having in the sixth grade?

Thomas Merton Despairs of His Path. Thomas Merton was raised as a nominal Protestant, but in a family where God was relegated to the sidelines of life. When he entered adulthood, he had little or no religious faith. But over time he began to understand this as a void in his life, and he began to show a deep hunger for spiritual direction. He was eventually led to the Catholic Church, where he became a Trappist monk. But before reaching that point he had to first find out for himself that happiness only comes when we "seek first the kingdom." He tells his story in his autobiographical book, *The Seven Storey Mountain:*

"Here I was, scarcely four years after I had left Oakham and walked out into the world that I thought I was going to ransack and rob of all its pleasures and satisfactions. I had done what I had intended, and now I found that it was I who was emptied and robbed and gutted. What a strange thing! In filling myself, I had emptied myself. In grasping things, I had lost everything. In devouring pleasures and joys, I had found distress and anguish and fear. And now, finally, as a piece of poetic justice, when I was reduced to this extremity of misery and humiliation, I fell into a love affair in which I was at last treated in the way I had treated not a few people in these last years.

"This girl lived on my own street, and I had the privilege of seeing her drive off with my rivals ten minutes after she had flatly refused to go out with me, asserting that she was tired and wanted to stay home. She did not even bother to conceal the fact that she found me amusing when there was nothing better to occupy her mind. She used to regale me with descriptions of what she considered to be a good time, and of the kind of people she admired and liked—they were precisely the shallow and superficial ones that gave me gooseflesh when I saw them sitting around in the Stork Club. And it was the will of God that for my just punishment I should take all this in the most abject meekness, and sit and beg like some kind of a pet dog until I finally got a pat on the head or some small sign of affection.

"... I came out of it chastened and abject, though not nearly as abject as I ought to have been and returned to the almost equal humiliation of my quarts of ice-cream.

"Such was the death of the hero, the great man I had wanted to be. ..."[1]

WEEK 10: LAST EPIPHANY

A Light for Action
Matthew 7:21–29

 **GATHERING** 10 min.    **STUDY** 30 min.    **CARING** 20–40 min.

Leader: The agenda has three parts. In the Gathering time you'll be getting to know each other through an "ice-breaker." This will be for your total group. The Study time has two parts: (1) Story and (2) Scripture. If you are short of time, skip the Story and move to the Scripture. Begin by reading out loud the Story or the Scripture to the whole group. Then divide into groups of 4 for the Study time. Finally, regather the total group for the Caring time. Keep to this agenda: (1) Gathering—10 minutes, (2) Study—30 minutes, and (3) Caring—20–40 minutes.

 **Irresistible Bargains.** When money is tight, many of us look for the bargains! Go around and let each person answer the first question. Then go around on the second question.

1. Which of the following bargains would you have the greatest trouble resisting? Choose your top two.
   - ❏ 30% off sale on fine gourmet chocolates
   - ❏ "second entree free" coupon at a romantic restaurant
   - ❏ free airline ticket to Las Vegas
   - ❏ 2-for-1 sale in the clothing department of your favorite store
   - ❏ box seats at general admission prices for your favorite team
   - ❏ fine piece of antique furniture going for 2/3 listed value at an auction
   - ❏ chance to get tickets for the live performance of your favorite singer or band for half-price

2. Mark where you would fall on the following continuum. "When it comes to bargains, I am generally ..."

1	2	3	4	5
cynical	suspicious	cautious	receptive	ready & eager!

PURPOSE

To understand that the light God gives us should lead to action on our part.

FOR THE PASTOR

The following material you can use as input for your sermon preparation on this week's Gospel Scripture from the book of Matthew. For further input you may want to share and further comment on the story of Mother Teresa, which your study group(s) will be responding to during their session. Also, it's important to share in your sermon or homily your own response to the personal question (or other personally-oriented question) to model personal sharing for your congregation.

SCRIPTURE

[21] *"Not everyone who says to me, 'Lord, Lord,' will enter the kingdom of heaven, but only the one who does the will of my Father in heaven.* [22] *On that day many will say to me, 'Lord, Lord, did we not prophesy in your name, and cast out demons in your name, and do many deeds of power in your name?'* [23] *Then I will declare to them, 'I never knew you; go away from me, you evildoers.'*

[24] *"Everyone then who hears these words of mine and acts on them will be like a wise man who built his house on rock.* [25] *The rain fell, the floods came, and the winds blew and beat on that house, but it did not fall, because it had been founded on rock.* [26] *And everyone who hears these words of mine and does not act on them will be like a foolish man who built his house on sand.* [27] *The rain fell, and the floods came, and the winds blew and beat against that house, and it fell—and great was its fall!"*

[28] *Now when Jesus had finished saying these things, the crowds were astounded at his teaching,* [29] *for he taught them as one having authority, and not as their scribes.*

Matthew 7:21–29

INTRODUCTION

"Lights! Camera! Action!" With those words the filming of movies begins. And it is the action that makes a movie exciting. Whether the action is the car-crashing, sometimes violent happenings in the so-called "action movies", or the plottings of Robin Williams to get his kids back in "Mrs. Doubtfire," a movie that enthralls us will have to get beyond talk to action. That is also true with the life of one who seeks to follow Christ. We can say all sorts of beautiful sayings, quoting the most eloquent of Scriptures, but if we are not acting on those beautiful sayings ourselves, then no one will really listen or respond. Even more tragically, we will never really be in communion with God ourselves. Not all of us will show our faith with the same actions. Some may choose to be involved in a project that helps the poor. Others will go on a lay witness mission to another church. Still others will get involved politically on an issue to which their faith speaks. But whichever form of action we take, the necessity of action is central to our life and witness as Christians.

7:21 *'Lord, Lord.'* The earliest Christian confession was "Jesus is Lord" (1 Corinthians 12:3). Jesus was pointing out that such a confession was not enough if not accompanied by action. He makes the same point again in Luke 6:46 where he says, "Why do you call me 'Lord, Lord,' and do not do what I tell you?"

7:22 *On that day.* This refers to the Day of Judgment (see Isaiah 2:11 and Zechariah 14:6 for other instances of this phrase being used in this way). *did we not.* Here the hypothetical defense refers to actual actions, but what kind of actions are they? They are acts of power, not acts of love or obedient faith.

7:24 *on rock.* Houses whose foundations were secured to bedrock would be able to survive a bad storm. In this saying Jesus is very close to a rabbinical saying found in the Aboth R. Nathan which reads: "A man who has works and has learnt much Torah, to what may he be likened? To a man who builds below with stones and above with adobe; and when much water comes and surrounds it, the stones are not moved from their place. But a man who has no good works and learns Torah, to what may he be likened? To a man who builds first with adobe and then with stones, and when even small streams come, they are immediately toppled over."[1]

7:26 *on sand.* The Holy Land has many "wadis," which are riverbeds that dry up in the summer, leaving a smooth riverbed of sand. The smooth bed would make for easy building, but when the rains come, that bed can turn into a raging river!

7:29 *their scribes.* These were people who interpreted Jewish religious law. Originally, it was their job to make copies of the Old Testament. Because of their familiarity with Scripture, people consulted them about points of law, and hence their role evolved into that of "teacher of the law." Their authority rested on their ability to quote the writings of earlier rabbis to prove their points. In contrast, Jesus' power lay in his message's implicit moral force and in the fact that he called upon no outside authority to validate his teaching.

Of all the houses you've lived in, which is your favorite? What did you particularly like about it? What was it made out of?

Mother Teresa Teaches About God. Mother Teresa is known throughout the world for the work she did with the poorest of the poor in Calcutta, India. But what many don't know is that she also established similar ministries with the poor around the world. In one work set up at Palermo in Sicily, the way that Mother Teresa and her Sisters taught about Christ through action has helped people feel like part of a caring family. Lush Gjergji tells the story in *Mother Teresa: Her Life, Her Works:*

"Not long ago I visited the Sisters at Palermo. The poor section is right in the center of the old city. Next to the crumbling buildings I found the convent, where six missionaries live today. This convent has become a new oasis of love and Christian witness. There the Sisters take care of forty old people, abandoned without anyone to love or care for them.

"During our conversation one of the old men told me: 'This old quarter of poor people isn't poor any longer. For us it has become a corner of the earthly paradise. My own children abandoned me; they say they have their own careers (one is a doctor), but neither God nor these Sisters abandoned me.' ...

"When faced with certain repulsive sights, one instinctively pulls back, and begins to wonder whether one can really help. I asked the Sisters how they felt when they found themselves here. They told me:

" 'At first it was rather difficult. People here live in isolation; they hardly see any reason to keep on living at all. Obviously, they have only the haziest ideas about God. With our witness and our affection we woke them from their torpor, and gave them something to think about in connection with human values. By now both they and we have grasped that many things can be changed. The improvement is obvious. Our little children are very easily distinguished from the rest. There is still much to be done among them, with the young people, with the families, and on the parish level. But even in the long range programs things have begun to move. Let us hope. ...' "[2]

[1]From *The Interpreter's Bible*, ed. George Buttrick Vol. 7: New Testament Articles—Matthew and Mark (Nashville: Abingdon Press, 1951), p. 334.
[2]Lush Gjergji, *Mother Teresa: Her Life, Her Works* (Hyde Park, NY: New City Press, 1991), pp. 88–89.

SPRING SEASON
LENT

Theme: "Standing Up to the Tests"

SERENDIPITY

Small Group
HANDOUT

WEEK 1: LENT 1
Tests of Temptation
Matthew 4:1–11

 GATHERING
10 min.

 STUDY
30 min.

 CARING
20–40 min.

Leader: The agenda has three parts. In the Gathering time you'll be getting to know each other through an "ice-breaker." This will be for your total group. The Study time has two parts: (1) Story and (2) Scripture. If you are short of time, skip the Story and move to the Scripture. Begin by reading out loud the Story or the Scripture to the whole group. Then divide into groups of 4 for the Study time. Finally, regather the total group for the Caring time. Keep to this agenda: (1) Gathering—10 minutes, (2) Study—30 minutes, and (3) Caring—20–40 minutes.

 **The Old Neighborhood.** Use the questions below to get acquainted. Go around the group on the first question. Then go around on the second question.

1. Was the "old neighborhood" where you grew up more like ...
   - ❏ Sesame Street—urban and multicultural
   - ❏ Bill Cosby's neighborhood—distinctively ethnic
   - ❏ Home Improvement—suburban housing with a common cultural background
   - ❏ The Waltons—rural and spread out, but closeknit

2. Choose as many of the following to share as you have time for:
   - Where did the kids gather in your neighborhood?
   - What were your favorite activities to do together?
   - Where were the special places—best climbing trees, best fishing holes? Places you could go to hide from adults?
   - Where were the "danger spots"—yards with mean dogs, "Oscar the Grouches" who didn't seem to like people, "haunted" houses?

<table>
<tr><td>SESSION
1</td><td><h1>Tests Of Temptation</h1>
Lent 1 - Matthew 4:1–11</td></tr>
</table>

PURPOSE

To see how Jesus stood up to the tests of temptation, and how he can help us to do the same.

FOR THE PASTOR

The following material you can use as input for your sermon preparation on this week's Gospel Scripture from the book of Matthew. For further input you may want to share and further comment on the story of Corrie ten Boom, which your study group(s) will be responding to during their session. Also, it's important to share in your sermon or homily your own response to the personal question (or other personally-oriented question) to model personal sharing for your congregation.

SCRIPTURE

4 **Then Jesus was led up by the Spirit into the wilderness to be tempted by the devil. [2]He fasted forty days and forty nights, and afterwards he was famished. [3]The tempter came and said to him, "If you are the Son of God, command these stones to become loaves of bread." [4]But he answered, "It is written,**

> **'One does not live by bread alone,**
>> **but by every word that comes from the mouth of God.' "**

[5]Then the devil took him to the holy city and placed him on the pinnacle of the temple, [6]saying to him, "If you are the Son of God, throw yourself down; for it is written,

> **'He will command his angels concerning you,**
>> **and 'On their hands they will bear you up,**
> **so that you will not dash your foot against a stone.' "**

[7]Jesus said to him, "Again it is written, 'Do not put the Lord your God to the test.' "

[8]Again, the devil took him to a very high mountain and showed him all the kingdoms of the world and their splendor; [9]and he said to him, "All these I will give you, if you will fall down and worship me." [10]Jesus said to him, "Away with you, Satan! for it is written,

> **'Worship the Lord your God,**
>> **and serve only him.' "**

[11]Then the devil left him, and suddenly angels came and waited on him.

Matthew 4:1–11

Before Jesus went out to teach and minister, he went through a time of intense temptation where he was tempted to think primarily of himself. We cannot assume this is the only time he went through such temptation, but this must have been a particularly difficult one. He voluntarily went out alone into the desert to meditate on himself and his role in God's plan. It was doubtlessly a time of struggle for him, and the temptations we are told about focused on his entire life direction. He was tempted to focus his power on serving himself and Satan, but his response in this story, as well as through the actions of the rest of his life, was to commit himself to serving God and God's children.

NOTES ON THE TEXT

4:1 *tempted.* This word always means "test" in Matthew. This was a trial of strength in which Satan's intent was to get Jesus to renounce his identity as the anointed Son of God.

4:2 *forty days.* Moses fasted forty days on Mount Sinai while receiving the commandments (Exodus 34:28), and Israel was in the wilderness forty years (Deuteronomy 8:2). Matthew pictures Jesus as the new Moses, and his followers as the new Israel.

4:3 *bread.* Satan's suggestion is not evil in itself, but in the context of this test, it would be like Israel's complaining that God had not adequately met their needs in the desert (Exodus 16). Rather than trust God, the temptation is for Jesus to take matters into his own hands.

4:4 *It is written ...* Note that Jesus always answers from Scripture. Here he refers to Deuteronomy 8:3.

4:5 *the pinnacle of the temple.* Bible scholar William Barclay says this would have been a point about 450 feet above the Kidron Valley. The temple was the focal point in Israel of God's love and power. The challenge is to prove this love and power by creating a peril from which only God could rescue him. This would be using his power in a way to manipulate God, and would be using God's power presumptuously.

4:6 *for it is written ...* Satan now quotes Psalm 91:11–12 to prove his case, which just goes to show that even Satan can quote Scripture! Satan misapplies a promise of God's protection to get Jesus to do something that would be foolhardy.

4:7 Jesus recognizes the manipulative tactic of Satan and responds with a quote from Deuteronomy 6:16.

4:10 Jesus quotes Deuteronomy 6:13 to affirm his allegiance to God and to reject Satan's offer. Satan had appealed to Jesus' legitimate needs (v. 3), his insecurities (vv. 6–7), and his ambitions (v. 8), but had failed to overcome Jesus' loyalty to God.

PERSONAL QUESTION

If you had to live on one kind of food alone, what kind of food would you choose?

STORY

Corrie ten Boom's Temptations. Corrie ten Boom was a devout Christian woman whose family sheltered Jews from the Nazis during the occupation of her native Holland. She and other members of her family, including her sister Betsie, were eventually arrested, and they had to endure a series of concentration camps. She tells her story in one of the great modern spiritual autobiographies, *The Hiding Place.* In the following segment she tells of the temptations she faced after many months, and now in Ravensbruck, one of the most infamous of all camps:

"And as the cold increased, so did the special temptation of concentration-camp life: the temptation to think only of oneself. It took a thousand cunning forms. I quickly discovered that when I maneuvered our way toward the middle of the roll-call formation we had a little protection from the wind.

"I knew this was self-centered: when Betsie and I stood at the center, someone else had to stand on the edge. How easy it was to give it other names! I was acting only for Betsie's sake. We were in an important ministry and must keep well. It was colder in Poland than in Holland; these Polish women were not feeling the chill the way we were.

"Selfishness had a life of its own. As I watched Mien's bag of yeast-compound [a vitamin compound they shared] disappear I began taking it from beneath the straw only after lights-out when others would not see and ask for some. Wasn't Betsie's health more important? ...

"And even if it wasn't right—it wasn't so *very* wrong, was it? Not wrong like sadism and murder and the other monstrous evils we saw in Ravensbruck every day. Oh, this was the great ploy of Satan in that kingdom of his: to display such blatant evil that one could almost believe one's own secret sins didn't matter.

"The cancer spread. The second week in December, every occupant of Barracks 28 was issued an extra blanket. The next day a large group of evacuees arrived from Czechoslovakia. One of them assigned to our platform had no blanket at all and Betsie insisted that we give her one of ours. So that evening I 'lent' her a blanket. But I didn't 'give' it to her. In my heart I held onto the right to that blanket."[1]

[1]Corrie ten Boom, *The Hiding Place* (Minneapolis, MN: World Wide Publications, 1971), pp. 211–212.

WEEK 2: LENT 2
Tests of Eternal Vision
John 3:1–17

 **GATHERING**
10 min.

 **STUDY**
30 min.

 **CARING**
20–40 min.

Leader: The agenda has three parts. In the Gathering time you'll be getting to know each other through an "ice-breaker." This will be for your total group. The Study time has two parts: (1) Story and (2) Scripture. If you are short of time, skip the Story and move to the Scripture. Begin by reading out loud the Story or the Scripture to the whole group. Then divide into groups of 4 for the Study time. Finally, regather the total group for the Caring time. Keep to this agenda: (1) Gathering—10 minutes, (2) Study—30 minutes, and (3) Caring—20–40 minutes.

 **Bring Out Your Best!** Use the questions below to get better acquainted. Go around the group on the first question. Then go around on the next question, etc.

1. Finish this sentence: If you want to bring out my best, then ..."
    - ❒ put me around playful people   ❒ give me lots of hugs
    - ❒ compliment my appearance   ❒ give me a challenge
    - ❒ put me in a competitive situation   ❒ feed me
    - ❒ give me a charge card and send me to the mall

2. Finish this sentence: "If you want to bring out my worst ..."
    - ❒ put me in a competitive situation   ❒ criticize me
    - ❒ try putting me on a committee   ❒ try telling me what to do
    - ❒ put me in a messy room   ❒ make me eat health food
    - ❒ give me a charge card and send me to the mall

<table>
<tr><td>SESSION
2</td><td><h1>Tests of Eternal Vision</h1>Lent 2 - John 3:1–17</td></tr>
</table>

PURPOSE

To consider how one test of a leader is whether they have a vision that goes beyond the present moment, and to see how Jesus stood up to that test of an eternal vision.

FOR THE PASTOR

The following material you can use as input for your sermon preparation on this week's Gospel Scripture from the book of John. For further input you may want to share and further comment on the story of St. Francis of Assisi, which your study group(s) will be responding to during their session. Also, it's important to share in your sermon or homily your own response to the personal question (or other personally-oriented question) to model personal sharing for your congregation.

SCRIPTURE

3 *Now there was a Pharisee named Nicodemus, a leader of the Jews. [2]He came to Jesus by night and said to him, "Rabbi, we know that you are a teacher who has come from God; for no one can do these signs that you do apart from the presence of God." [3]Jesus answered him, "Very truly, I tell you, no one can see the kingdom of God without being born from above." [4]Nicodemus said to him, "How can anyone be born after having grown old? Can one enter a second time into the mother's womb and be born?" [5]Jesus answered, "Very truly, I tell you, no one can enter the kingdom of God without being born of water and Spirit. [6]What is born of the flesh is flesh, and what is born of the Spirit is spirit. [7]Do not be astonished that I said to you, 'You must be born from above.' [8]The wind blows where it chooses, and you hear the sound of it, but you do not know where it comes from or where it goes. So it is with everyone who is born of the Spirit." [9]Nicodemus said to him, "How can these things be?" [10]Jesus answered him, "Are you a teacher of Israel, and yet you do not understand these things?"*

[11]"Very truly, I tell you, we speak of what we know and testify to what we have seen; yet you do not receive our testimony. [12]If I have told you about earthly things and you do not believe, how can you believe if I tell you about heavenly things? [13]No one has ascended into heaven except the one who descended from heaven, the Son of Man. [14]And just as Moses lifted up the serpent in the wilderness, so must the Son of Man be lifted up, [15]that whoever believes in him may have eternal life.

[16]"For God so loved the world that he gave his only Son, so that everyone who believes in him may not perish but may have eternal life.

[17]"Indeed, God did not send the Son into the world to condemn the world, but in order that the world might be saved through him."

John 3:1–17

The phrase "born again" has become somewhat of a divisive one in the church. Some people use it as a means of separating themselves from other Christians. They, as opposed to others who call themselves Christians, are "born again" Christians. The message that some have received in this is that unless one has "come forward" in an emotion-ladened experience where one has turned their life around, one is not legitimately Christian. As we read this story, however, we need to understand that regardless of the manner in which we have given ourselves to Christ, all persons who have done so are "born again." Some people have had emotional experiences. But some have just been raised in a strong Christian family, where their own commitment to Christ has been a process of growth over time. In either case, it is our response to the essential message of John 3:16 that determines our status—it is our belief that God does love us and sent his Son Jesus Christ to redeem us from sin's destruction that gives new life to our soul.

3:1 *Nicodemus*. Nicodemus, a respected religious authority, appears in John 7:50 and 19:39, but in no other Gospel. ***Pharisee.*** The Pharisees were a Jewish sect committed to the principle that religious and ethical purity was the means of securing God's favor. This in turn led to a concern for the fine points of the Jewish Law, which tended to overshadow the spirit of that Law. It was their narrow, legalistic approach to God and his Law that brought Jesus into conflict with them. ***a leader of the Jews.*** This means he was a member of the Sanhedrin. It was comprised of 71 members, and was presided over by the High Priest. Under Roman rule, the Sanhedrin's major function was to enforce Jewish customs. The Sanhedrin might recommend capital punishment, but did not have the authority to carry it out.

3:3 Jesus immediately moves the conversation to essential issues. ***born from above.*** Other versions say the better known "born again." "Born again" highlights the radical reorientation to life resulting from trusting Jesus, while "born from above" accents the reality that spiritual life is a gift from God, not something earned by virtue of one's performance.

3:5–8 Throughout this section there is a word-play between "wind" and "spirit" which is the same word in Greek, *pneuma*. ***being born of water and Spirit.*** Commentators differ on what is meant here: (1) Some think this phrase is a restatement of the call for a spiritual birth in addition to physical birth. Being born of water would refer to the "water-breaking" in physical birth; (2) Others assume that water represents the life-giving qualities of the Spirit (7:38–39); (3) Others think that the author, writing about A.D. 90–100, refers to contemporary practices of baptism as a symbol of baptism in the Spirit.

3:15 *eternal life*. This is the first use of a phrase seen over and over in this Gospel. Its meaning is not simply tied up with the quantity of time one exists, but much more with the quality of fullness, goodness and perfection of life with God.

3:16–17 These verses sum up the motive, the means, the extent, and the result of the whole Gospel story. Whereas the traditional Jewish faith spoke of God loving Israel, they never referred to his relationship with the whole world as one of love.

PERSONAL QUESTION

Nicodemus was a member of the Jewish ruling council. What are you a member of (or have you been a member of at some point in your life) that you are most proud of?

STORY

A Message for St. Francis. Francesco di Bernardone (Francis of Assisi) had been raised in a wealthy home where religion was a peripheral matter. But as he became his own person, he became more and more sensitive to a God who was claiming him as his own, as well as to the poor people of the land, with whom St. Francis had an empathy that has been unmatched since his time. Shortly after his conversion, he had a vision which was central. His biographer, Julien Green, tells of the experience in the book, *God's Fool: The Life and Times of Francis of Assisi:*

"One day when he was walking in the country, trying, like a good merchant, to get a clear picture of the situation, he pressed on as far as an ancient church that was falling into ruin, San Damiano. It was there that God had been waiting for him all along. A large, tragic crucifix, painted with touching naiveté, hung above the altar, and it caught his attention at once. The figure of Christ, with his arms outstretched, had a faraway look, as if his eyes were searching along the road for someone who had been long in coming. Francis immediately fell on his knees.

"In all Italy there were so many crucifixes, and from seeing them so often people had become blind to what the crosses were trying to say. But for Francis that day was not like any other day, and for the first time, perhaps, he saw the crucifixion. Then he had a sudden revelation of what the death of Jesus meant. It was as if no one had ever told him about it before, and his heart was torn with compassion and love, of love for the man who had let himself be nailed to the wood out of love for him, Francesco di Bernardone, now on his knees, speechless, his face wet with tears. ...

"[And a voice] said, 'Francis, repair my house.' From the heart of Christ to the heart of Francis love went back and forth in an indescribable exchange.

"When he came to, the young man experienced the desolation of the soul that finds itself back in the created world. After a moment he blessed himself and left, carrying away in his head a phrase he had misunderstood and in his heart the indelible imprint of the crucifixion. ... At last God had clearly revealed his will: He must repair the walls of his imperiled church. The only mistake lay in that lowercase 'c': he should have thought 'Church,' but how could he have?"[1]

[1]Julien Green, *God's Fool: The Life and Times of Francis of Assisi* (San Francisco: Harper & Row, 1983), pp. 70–71.

Small Group
HANDOUT

WEEK 3: LENT 3

Tests of Culture
John 4:5–30

 **GATHERING**
10 min.

 **STUDY**
30 min.

 **CARING**
20–40 min.

Leader: The agenda has three parts. In the Gathering time you'll be getting to know each other through an "ice-breaker." This will be for your total group. The Study time has two parts: (1) Story and (2) Scripture. If you are short of time, skip the Story and move to the Scripture. Begin by reading out loud the Story or the Scripture to the whole group. Then divide into groups of 4 for the Study time. Finally, regather the total group for the Caring time. Keep to this agenda: (1) Gathering—10 minutes, (2) Study—30 minutes, and (3) Caring—20–40 minutes.

 **Taking a "Stand."** With each of the following categories, stand up if they apply to you! (The group leader should read one at a time.):

- You would rather "channel surf" than "surf the Internet."

- You could tell what's currently happening in a daytime "soap."

- You like your driver's license photo.

- The first newspaper section you read is not the comic or the sports section.

- You sometimes watch *Sesame Street* when no children are around.

- You have not gotten a call from a telemarketer this week.

- You like eating sushi.

- You sometimes sneak a snack when no one is looking.

- You always drive under the speed limit.

Tests of Culture
Lent 3 - John 4:5–30

PURPOSE

To consider how Jesus stood up to the test of being able to speak across cultures.

FOR THE PASTOR

The following material you can use as input for your sermon preparation on this week's Gospel Scripture from the book of John. For further input you may want to share and further comment on the story of Albert Schweitzer, which your study group(s) will be responding to during their session. Also, it's important to share in your sermon or homily your own response to the personal question (or other personally-oriented question) to model personal sharing for your congregation.

SCRIPTURE

⁵So he came to a Samaritan city called Sychar, near the plot of ground that Jacob had given to his son Joseph. ⁶Jacob's well was there, and Jesus, tired out by his journey, was sitting by the well. It was about noon.

⁷A Samaritan woman came to draw water, and Jesus said to her, "Give me a drink." ⁸(His disciples had gone to the city to buy food.) ⁹The Samaritan woman said to him, "How is it that you, a Jew, ask a drink of me, a woman of Samaria?" (Jews do not share things in common with Samaritans.) ¹⁰Jesus answered her, "If you knew the gift of God, and who it is that is saying to you, 'Give me a drink,' you would have asked him, and he would have given you living water." ¹¹The woman said to him, "Sir, you have no bucket, and the well is deep. Where do you get that living water? ¹²Are you greater than our ancestor Jacob, who gave us the well, and with his sons and his flocks drank from it?" ¹³Jesus said to her, "Everyone who drinks of this water will be thirsty again, ¹⁴but those who drink of the water that I will give them will never be thirsty. The water that I will give will become in them a spring of water gushing up to eternal life." ¹⁵The woman said to him, "Sir, give me this water, so that I may never be thirsty or have to keep coming here to draw water."

¹⁶Jesus said to her, "Go, call your husband and come back." ¹⁷The woman answered him, "I have no husband." Jesus said to her, "You are right in saying, 'I have no husband'; ¹⁸for you have had five husbands, and the one you have now is not your husband. What you have said is true!" ¹⁹The woman said to him, "Sir, I see that you are a prophet. ²⁰Our ancestors worshiped on this mountain, but you say that the place where people must worship is in Jerusalem." ²¹Jesus said to her, "Woman, believe me, the hour is coming when you will worship the Father neither on this mountain nor in Jerusalem. ²²You worship what you do not know; we worship what we know, for salvation is from the Jews. ²³But the hour is coming, and is now here, when the true worshipers will worship the Father in spirit and truth, for the Father seeks such as these to worship him. ²⁴God is spirit, and those who worship him must worship in spirit and truth." ²⁵The woman said to him, "I know that Messiah is coming" (who is called Christ). "When he comes, he will proclaim all things to us." ²⁶Jesus said to her, "I am he, the one who is speaking to you."

²⁷Just then his disciples came. They were astonished that he was speaking with a woman, but no one said, "What do you want?" or "Why are you speaking with her?" ²⁸Then the woman left her water jar and went back to the city. She said to the people, ²⁹"Come and see a man who told me everything I have ever done! He cannot be the Messiah, can he?" ³⁰They left the city and were on their way to him.

John 4:5–30 (full lectionary reference: John 4:5–42)

INTRODUCTION

Many people in the world tie Christ and Christianity to Western culture, particularly the cultures of the United States and Europe. But what they forget is that Christianity arose in the Semitic culture of the Middle East. In addition, what many don't realize is that Christianity is now growing fastest not in America or Europe, but in Africa. Christ has shown the ability to transcend cultures, and that is an important aspect of who he is. If a religion is based on principles or experiences that make sense only in a specific cultural mileau, then how valid can it be? But knowing that Christ speaks to people of many cultures assures us that he speaks to the common human experience and reveals a God who truly is the God of all of us as a human family.

NOTES ON THE TEXT

4:5 *the plot of ground* ... Genesis 48:22 tells of Jacob having given some land to his son Joseph.

4:7 *A Samaritan woman.* This woman represents all that was despised by the religiously pious of the Judaism of the day. Samaritans were a race hated by the Jews, and women were considered to be of much less value than men. In addition, we later find she is living an immoral life. ***came to draw water.*** Noontime, during the heat of the day, was not the time women would normally perform this chore. This woman probably came at this time to avoid meeting up with the "more respectable women."

4:9 *Jews do not share things in common* .... In particular a "good Jew" would not use the same cup or bucket such a person was using. Jesus' request shocks the woman. Her surprise may well be mixed with more than a touch of sarcasm.

4:10 *living water.* This was a common phrase meaning water that flowed from a river or spring. Water like this had better quality than the standing water of a well or pond. Jesus, however, is referring to spiritually "living water"—water that refreshes the soul.

4:17–18 While clearly revealing his knowledge of her situation, Jesus commends her truthfulness. Women at this time could be divorced for trivial reasons, but had no right of divorce themselves.

4:25 *Messiah.* The Samaritan's concept of the Messiah (based on Deut. 18:18) was less politically charged than that of the Jews. To the Samaritans the Messiah was the one who would restore true worship and teach of God as Moses had done. Given this contrast, Jesus could affirm this title for himself without fear of it being misinterpreted in political terms.

4:27 *speaking with a woman ...* One rabbinical saying cautioned a rabbi against talking even with his wife in public on account of what others, not knowing she was his wife, might say. The concern was not just with the rabbi's reputation, but with the fact that women were thought unworthy of being taught God's law.

<table>
<tr><td>

PERSONAL QUESTION

</td><td>

What would be the most difficult thing for you if you were to do what Albert Schweitzer did and go to another culture to care for people in Christ's name?

</td></tr>
<tr><td>

STORY

</td><td>

Albert Schweitzer in Africa. While Christianity is thriving in Africa today, it wasn't all that long ago when Christian missionary work in Africa was relatively new. Albert Schweitzer was part of that work. He grew up as the son of a prominent minister and had many talents that brought him recognition, including playing organ and writing theology. In addition to this he was an ordained minister! But then in his 30s he suddenly decided that he needed to give himself more to helping hurting people, and God wanted him to do this by getting a medical degree and caring for people in a remote section of equatorial Africa. In his autobiographical book, *Out of My Life and Thought*, he tells of some of this work:

</td></tr>
</table>

"An initial handicap in my work consisted in the difficulty of finding Africans who could serve as interpreters and helpers at the infirmary. The first who proved himself capable of assisting was a former cook by the name of Joseph Azoawani. He stayed with me, though I could not pay him as much as he had earned in his former job. He gave me some valuable hints about how to deal with the Africans, though I was unable to agree with the one he thought most important. He advised me to reject patients whose lives, so far as we could see, could not be saved. Again and again he held up to me the examples of fetishistic doctors who would have nothing to do with such cases so as to endanger as little as possible their reputation as healers.

"But on one point I later had to admit that he was right. When dealing with Africans, one must never hold out hope of their recovery to the patient and his relatives if the case is really hopeless. If death occurs without warning, they conclude that the doctor did not know that the disease would have this outcome because he had not diagnosed it correctly. One must tell the truth to African patients without reservation. They wish to know it, and they can bear it. Death for them is something natural. They are not afraid of it, but, on the contrary, face it calmly. If, against all expectations, the patient recovers, the doctor's reputation increases immensely. He is seen as one who can cure even fatal diseases."[1]

[1] Albert Schweitzer, *Out of My Life and Thought* (New York: Henry Holt & Co., 1949), pp. 138–139.

WEEK 4: LENT 4

Tests of Healing

John 9:1–30

 **GATHERING**
10 min.

 **STUDY**
30 min.

 **CARING**
20–40 min.

Leader: The agenda has three parts. In the Gathering time you'll be getting to know each other through an "ice-breaker." This will be for your total group. The Study time has two parts: (1) Story and (2) Scripture. If you are short of time, skip the Story and move to the Scripture. Begin by reading out loud the Story or the Scripture to the whole group. Then divide into groups of 4 for the Study time. Finally, regather the total group for the Caring time. Keep to this agenda: (1) Gathering—10 minutes, (2) Study—30 minutes, and (3) Caring—20–40 minutes.

 **A Different Kind of Medical History.** Any kind of group that you get involved in today seems to require you fill out a sheet on your medical history. So it seems we have been remiss! Look over the "highly scientific," but not so rare diseases below (with symptoms in parentheses), and mark the ones you have experienced:

☐ INTERNET-ITIS—staring at a monitor for hours while typing messages to people you've never met

☐ MONOTONE-EOSIS—causes people to move away from you like you have the plague when you sing *The Star Spangled Banner*

☐ CHOCO-HOLISM—snarling when people suggest you share your "chocolate decadence" dessert

☐ CHARGECARD-ITIS—a strong compulsion to hand plastic to anyone standing behind a store counter

☐ ESPN DEFICIENCY SYNDROME—going into convulsions when you haven't heard the sports scores in too long a time

☐ CHANNELSURF-EOSIS—cramps in your index finger from having to push the remote control buttons so much—often makes you bed or couch-ridden

Tests of Healing
Lent 4 - John 9:1–30

PURPOSE

To see how Jesus stood up to the tests of meeting people's needs for healing.

FOR THE PASTOR

The following material you can use as input for your sermon preparation on this week's Gospel Scripture from the book of John. For further input you may want to share and further comment on the story of Mother Teresa, which your study group(s) will be responding to during their session. Also, it's important to share in your sermon or homily your own response to the personal question (or other personally-oriented question) to model personal sharing for your congregation.

SCRIPTURE

9 *As he walked along, he saw a man blind from birth. ²His disciples asked him, "Rabbi, who sinned, this man or his parents, that he was born blind?" ³Jesus answered, "Neither this man nor his parents sinned; he was born blind so that God's works might be revealed in him. ⁴We must work the works of him who sent me while it is day; night is coming when no one can work. ⁵As long as I am in the world, I am the light of the world." ⁶When he had said this, he spat on the ground and made mud with the saliva and spread the mud on the man's eyes, ⁷saying to him, "Go, wash in the pool of Siloam" (which means Sent). Then he went and washed and came back able to see. ⁸The neighbors and those who had seen him before as a beggar began to ask, "Is this not the man who used to sit and beg?" ⁹Some were saying, "It is he." Others were saying, "No, but it is someone like him." He kept saying, "I am the man." ¹⁰But they kept asking him, "Then how were your eyes opened?" ¹¹He answered, "The man called Jesus made mud, spread it on my eyes, and said to me, 'Go to Siloam and wash.' Then I went and washed and received my sight." ¹²They said to him, "Where is he?" He said, "I do not know."*

¹³They brought to the Pharisees the man who had formerly been blind. ¹⁴Now it was a sabbath day when Jesus made the mud and opened his eyes. ¹⁵Then the Pharisees also began to ask him how he had received his sight. He said to them, "He put mud on my eyes. Then I washed, and now I see." ¹⁶Some of the Pharisees said, "This man is not from God, for he does not observe the sabbath." But others said, "How can a man who is a sinner perform such signs?" And they were divided. ¹⁷So they said again to the blind man, "What do you say about him? It was your eyes he opened." He said, "He is a prophet."

¹⁸The Jews did not believe that he had been blind and had received his sight until they called the parents of the man who had received his sight ¹⁹and asked them, "Is this your son, who you say was born blind? How then does he now see?" *[20]His parents answered, "We know that this is our son, and that he was born blind; [21]but we do not know how it is that now he sees, nor do we know who opened his eyes. Ask him; he is of age. He will speak for himself." [22]His parents said this because they were afraid of the Jews; for the Jews had already agreed that anyone who confessed Jesus to be the Messiah would be put out of the synagogue. [23]Therefore his parents said, "He is of age; ask him."*

[24]So for the second time they called the man who had been blind, and they said to him, "Give glory to God! We know that this man is a sinner." [25]He answered, "I do not know whether he is a sinner. One thing I do know, that though I was blind, now I see." [26]They said to him, "What did he do to you? How did he open your eyes? [27]He answered them, "I have told you already, and you would not listen. Why do you want to hear it again? Do you also want to become his disciples?" [28]Then they reviled him, saying, "You are his disciple, but we are disciples of Moses. [29]We know that God has spoken to Moses, but as for this man, we do not know where he comes from." [30]The man answered, "Here is an astonishing thing! You do not know where he comes from, and yet he opened my eyes. ..."

John 9:1–30 (full lectionary reference: John 9:1–41)

INTRODUCTION

We live in a world of wounded souls. Some of us are physically wounded, with injuries, diseases and disabilities that bring suffering to life and sometimes keep us from being all we could otherwise be. Others of us are emotionally wounded, with scars on our souls, sometimes from the wounds of a traumatic childhood, and sometimes from last week's divorce or relational conflict. Whatever the nature of our wounding, we seek healing. Physicians and counselors help with some of this today. But many times our wounding goes deeper than any human help can reach. It is in those times that we especially need the healing power of God. For many people today "faith healing" or "spiritual healing" has a bad name. They associate it with charlatans who take advantage of people's naiveté to receive glory (not to mention large sums of money!) for themselves. Certainly that happens. But from the very time of Christ's ministry and the ministry of the early church, many have found that through the power of Jesus Christ, God does bring healing to people in a way that steps beyond human understanding. That healing speaks strongly of who Christ was and the power of God manifested in him.

NOTES ON THE TEXT

9:2 *who sinned ...?* Note that the question is not *whether* someone sinned in order to deserve such a fate, but *who*. Despite the book of Job, the rabbis taught a person's misfortune was the result of his or her direct sin or a punishment inherited from one's parents' sins.

9:3 Jesus denies that blindness comes as a punishment for sin, but rather says that through such disabilities God can often show his glory by the way he uses the person for some good.

9:4 *night is coming.* His impending death will, for a time, quench the light of Christ.

9:6 *he spat.* People of this time believed that saliva had healing properties.

9:7 *the pool of Siloam.* The pool was near Jerusalem and was fed by canals from nearby springs. It was the pool from which water was drawn in the ceremonies associated with the Feast of Tabernacles, and was considered a place of purification.

9:13 *the Pharisees.* Judaism was divided into various sects along doctrinal, political, practical and social lines. The Pharisees were committed to the principle that religious and ethical purity was the means of securing God's favor. This in turn led to a concern for the fine points of the Jewish law which tended to overshadow the essence of that law.

9:14 *a sabbath day.* The Pharisees would have been particularly upset about Jesus healing on the sabbath day because healing was considered work, and you weren't supposed to work on the sabbath day.

9:21 *he is of age.* Legal age was 13 years old. The parents simply affirm he is old enough to speak for himself since they do not want to be implicated in anything that has happened.

PERSONAL QUESTION

Who is someone you admire because they have overcome a disability? How have they influenced your outlook on life?

STORY

The Healing Power of Love. There is perhaps no person in modern times who has been more respected and loved for their work with wounded and dying souls than Mother Teresa. She worked many years with "the poorest of the poor," and in particular people dying on the streets of Calcutta, India. Whenever God did not use her to bring actual physical healing, he at least used her to bring spiritual healing. On one occasion she shared a story of one person who was not poor. He developed leprosy, a disease that is much feared in India and for which tradition requires complete isolation from social contact. The story is retold in her biography by Lush Gjergji:

"Let me tell you about an incident that happened. A very rich and distinguished man perceived that he had contracted leprosy. Right away he had to give up his family and his important job in the company. His wife had insisted on this: 'You know very well that if you do not leave the house our daughters will never be able to marry. So, go away.' He obeyed and sought asylum in a refuge for the poor. He asked for nothing, not even medical attention: he just wanted to die in peace. One day our Sisters found him; they disinfected his sores and placed him in a bed. That day he changed, and said: 'Now I believe that God really loves me.'

Today he is our best helper in all our undertakings, in assistance to the sick and in our school work. He has changed completely and was really born again when he realized that he was loved."[1]

[1] Lush Gjergi, *Mother Teresa: Her Life, Her Works* (Hyde Park, NY: New City Press, 1991), p. 64.

Small Group
HANDOUT

WEEK 5: LENT 5

Tests of Power Over Death
John 11:1–7,17–45

 **GATHERING**
10 min.

 **STUDY**
30 min.

 **CARING**
20–40 min.

Leader: The agenda has three parts. In the Gathering time you'll be getting to know each other through an "ice-breaker." This will be for your total group. The Study time has two parts: (1) Story and (2) Scripture. If you are short of time, skip the Story and move to the Scripture. Begin by reading out loud the Story or the Scripture to the whole group. Then divide into groups of 4 for the Study time. Finally, regather the total group for the Caring time. Keep to this agenda: (1) Gathering—10 minutes, (2) Study—30 minutes, and (3) Caring—20–40 minutes.

 **Assessing the Future.** Go around and let each person answer one of the questions below, or both.

1. Which phrase would best describe your philosophy about facing the future?
    - ❑ "I don't want to grow up!"
    - ❑ "Back to the future!"
    - ❑ "You can't go home again."
    - ❑ "One day at a time, sweet Jesus."
    - ❑ "He who isn't busy being born is busy dying."
    - ❑ "The future belongs to those who plan for it."
    - ❑ "I don't know what the future holds, but I know who holds the future."
    - ❑ "Every day in every way, things are getting better."
    - ❑ "The future's so bright, I've got to wear shades!"

2. Finish this sentence: "One thing that I'll have in the future which I do not have now is ..."

Tests of Power Over Death
Lent 5 - John 11:1–7,17–45

PURPOSE

To see how Christ stands up to the test of helping us deal with death and the fear of death.

FOR THE PASTOR

The following material you can use as input for your sermon preparation on this week's Gospel Scripture from the book of John. For further input you may want to share and further comment on the story of Thomas Merton, which your study group(s) will be responding to during their session. Also, it's important to share in your sermon or homily your own response to the personal question (or other personally-oriented question) to model personal sharing for your congregation.

SCRIPTURE

11 *Now a certain man was ill, Lazarus of Bethany, the village of Mary and her sister Martha. ²Mary was the one who anointed the Lord with perfume and wiped his feet with her hair; her brother Lazarus was ill. ³So the sisters sent a message to Jesus, "Lord, he whom you love is ill." ⁴But when Jesus heard it, he said, "This illness does not lead to death; rather it is for God's glory, so that the Son of God may be glorified through it." ⁵Accordingly, though Jesus loved Martha and her sister and Lazarus, ⁶after having heard that Lazarus was ill, he stayed two days longer in the place where he was.*

⁷Then after this he said to the disciples, "Let us go to Judea again." ...

¹⁷When Jesus arrived, he found that Lazarus had already been in the tomb four days. ¹⁸Now Bethany was near Jerusalem, some two miles away, ¹⁹and many of the Jews had come to Martha and Mary to console them about their brother. ²⁰When Martha heard that Jesus was coming, she went and met him, while Mary stayed at home. ²¹Martha said to Jesus, "Lord, if you had been here, my brother would not have died. ²²But even now I know that God will give you whatever you ask of him." ²³Jesus said to her, "Your brother will rise again." ²⁴Martha said to him, "I know that he will rise again in the resurrection on the last day." ²⁵Jesus said to her, "I am the resurrection and the life. Those who believe in me, even though they die, will live, ²⁶and everyone who lives and believes in me will never die. Do you believe this? ²⁷She said to him, "Yes, Lord, I believe that you are the Messiah, the Son of God, the one coming into the world."

²⁸When she had said this, she went back and called her sister Mary, and told her privately, "The Teacher is here and is calling for you." ²⁹And when she heard it, she got up quickly and went to him. ³⁰Now Jesus had not yet come to the village, but was still at the place where Martha had met him. ³¹The Jews who were with her in the house, consoling her, saw Mary get up quickly and go out. They followed her because they thought that she was going to the tomb to weep there. ³²When Mary came where Jesus was and saw him, she knelt at his feet and said to him, "Lord, if you had been here, my brother would not have died." ³³When Jesus saw her weeping, and the Jews who came with her also weeping, he was greatly disturbed in spirit and deeply moved. ³⁴He said, "Where have you laid him?" They said to him, "Lord, come and see." ³⁵Jesus began to weep. ³⁶So the Jews said, "See how he loved him!" ³⁷But some of them said, "Could not he who opened the eyes of the blind man have kept this man from dying?"

³⁸Then Jesus, again greatly disturbed, came to the tomb. It was a cave, and a stone was lying against it. ³⁹Jesus said, "Take away the stone." Martha, the sister of the dead man, said to him, "Lord, already there is a stench because he has been dead four days." ⁴⁰Jesus said to her, "Did I not tell you that if you believed, you would see the glory of God?" ⁴¹So they took away the stone. And Jesus looked upward and said, "Father, I thank you for having heard me. ⁴²I knew that you always hear me, but I have said this for the sake of the crowd standing here, so that they may believe that you sent me." ⁴³When he had said this, he cried with a loud voice, "Lazarus, come out!" ⁴⁴The dead man came out, his hands and feet bound with strips of cloth, and his face wrapped in a cloth. Jesus said to them, "Unbind him, and let him go."

⁴⁵Many of the Jews therefore, who had come with Mary and had seen what Jesus did, believed in him.

John 11:1–7,17–45 (full lectionary reference: John 11:1–45)

<table>
<tr><td>INTRODUCTION</td><td>

We live in a society that seeks to deny death. We send our older people to nursing homes or hospitals so they can die out of view. Cosmetics, hair coloring and cosmetic surgery to erase the signs of aging are all high-profit industries. And anyone who talks about death to any degree is generally referred to as "morbid." Some even are seeking to avoid death more completely by investing in cryonics—freezing themself after death with a belief that at some future time they can be revived. In the midst of this death-denial, we experience Lent, the time when we remember Jesus' march toward his death by crucifixion in Jerusalem. For a death-denying society, having a person die such a death is the ultimate sign of defeat— it's being defeated by our ultimate enemy. But the Good News of Jesus Christ is that he turned the cross into a sign of victory. He approached death undeterred by its power, faced it in obedience to his heavenly Father, and came out victorious over it by rising from the dead! While death is for many a sign of failure, it became the ultimate sign that Jesus had really stood up to all the tests of being a special person from God. Lent can be a time when we share in that victory if we stop denying death, and face it with acceptance and hope through Jesus Christ.

</td></tr>
<tr><td>NOTES ON THE TEXT</td><td>

11:2 *Mary.* The author, aware that the story of Jesus' anointing was a familiar one to his readers, used this incident to identify Mary even though it doesn't occur in this Gospel until chapter 12.

11:6 *two days longer.* At least two views are possible as to why he did this: (1) Jesus simply ignored an urgent request to act in a needy situa-

</td></tr>
</table>

tion, and in so doing communicated that his agenda is set neither by himself, nor by the desires of those he loves, but by the Father; (2) He waited in order that through this trial his glory would be revealed in a new way.

11:17 *four days.* Since Jesus' journey was probably only a day's length at most, Lazarus must have died the day Jesus received the message. There was a notion that up until the third day a person's spirit hovered over the body, allowing for the hope of recovery, but after that no hope was possible. Jesus' delay may have been to disavow any expectation that recovery could be possible, according to their normal expectations. Mourning ceremonies reached their crescendo on the fourth day.

PERSONAL QUESTION

When have you had to deal with a difficult loss of a loved one, like Thomas Merton did in the story below?

STORY

The Death of Thomas Merton's Father. Thomas Merton grew up in a family that was nominally Protestant, but really had little religious faith. When he became an adult, however, he began to be torn by religious questions, and eventually was attracted to Catholicism and became not only a priest, but a Trappist monk. In the story of his spiritual pilgrimage, *The Seven Storey Mountain,* he tells how it was when he was still a non-believer and had to confront the reality that his father was dying. He writes:

"We went into the ward. Father was in bed, to the left, just as you went in the door.

"And when I saw him, I knew there was no hope of him living much longer. His face was swollen. His eyes were not clear but, above all, the tumor had raised a tremendous swelling on his forehead.

"I said: 'How are you, Father?'

"He looked at me and put forth his hand, in a confused and unhappy way, and I realized he could no longer even speak. But at the same time, you could see that he knew us, and knew what was going on, and that his mind was clear, and that he understood everything.

"But the sorrow of his great helplessness suddenly fell upon me like a mountain. I was crushed by it. The tears sprang to my eyes. Nobody said anything more.

"I hid my face in the blanket and cried. And poor father wept, too. The others stood by. It was excruciatingly sad. We were completely helpless. There was nothing anyone could do. ...

"What could I make of so much suffering? There was no way for me, or for anyone else in the family, to get anything out of it. It was a raw wound for which there was no adequate relief. You had to take it, like an animal. ... Try to avoid it, if you could. But you must eventually reach the point where you can't avoid it any more. Take it. Try to stupefy yourself, if you like, so that it won't hurt so much. But you will always have to take some of it. And it will all devour you in the end."[1]

Small Group
HANDOUT

WEEK 6: LENT 6
Tests of Faithfulness
Matthew 27:11–18,20–23,26–31,33–46,50,54

 **GATHERING**
10 min.

 **STUDY**
30 min.

 **CARING**
20–40 min.

Leader: The agenda has three parts. In the Gathering time you'll be getting to know each other through an "ice-breaker." This will be for your total group. The Study time has two parts: (1) Story and (2) Scripture. If you are short of time, skip the Story and move to the Scripture. Begin by reading out loud the Story or the Scripture to the whole group. Then divide into groups of 4 for the Study time. Finally, regather the total group for the Caring time. Keep to this agenda: (1) Gathering—10 minutes, (2) Study—30 minutes, and (3) Caring—20–40 minutes.

 **Everyday Blessings.** Have everyone in your group think of the person on their left. Choose an everyday object, such as you might find around your home, that reminds you of a special quality that person has. Use one of the examples below, or come up with your own:

PAPER CLIP: You have helped hold the group together.

LIGHT BULB: You light up the room.

ELECTRICAL OUTLET: You are full of power and energy.

TELEPHONE: You help people communicate.

WINDOW: You help us see things a little more clearly.

EASY CHAIR: You help us all relax.

POTPOURRI: You bring freshness and a nice atmosphere.

FIREPLACE: You bring warmth and coziness.

Tests of Faithfulness

Lent 6 - Matthew 27:11–18,20–23,26–31,33–46,50,54

PURPOSE

To take a look at how Jesus showed faithfulness in going to the Cross, and to learn to follow his example.

FOR THE PASTOR

The following material you can use as input for your sermon preparation on this week's Gospel Scripture from the book of Matthew. For further input you may want to share and further comment on the story of Corrie ten Boom, which your study group(s) will be responding to during their session. Also, it's important to share in your sermon or homily your own response to the personal question (or other personally-oriented question) to model personal sharing for your congregation.

SCRIPTURE

[11]Now Jesus stood before the governor; and the governor asked him, "Are you the King of the Jews?" Jesus said, "You say so." [12]But when he was accused by the chief priests and elders, he did not answer. [13]Then Pilate said to him, "Do you not hear how many accusations they make against you?" [14]But he gave him no answer, not even to a single charge, so that the governor was greatly amazed.

[15]Now at the festival the governor was accustomed to release a prisoner for the crowd, anyone whom they wanted. [16]At that time they had a notorious prisoner, called Jesus Barabbas. [17]So after they had gathered, Pilate said to them, "Whom do you want me to release for you, Jesus Barabbas or Jesus who is called the Messiah?" [18]For he realized that it was out of jealousy that they had handed him over. ... [20]Now the chief priests and the elders persuaded the crowds to ask for Barabbas and to have Jesus killed. [21]The governor again said to them, "Which of the two do you want me to release for you?" And they said, "Barabbas." [22]Pilate said to them, "Then what should I do with Jesus who is called the Messiah?" All of them said, "Let him be crucified!" [23]Then he asked, "Why, what evil has he done?" But they shouted all the more, "Let him be crucified!"

... [26]So he released Barabbas for them; and after flogging Jesus, he handed him over to be crucified.

[27]Then the soldiers of the governor took Jesus into the governor's headquarters, and they gathered the whole cohort around him. [28]They stripped him and put a scarlet robe on him, [29]and after twisting some thorns into a crown, they put it on his head. They put a reed in his right hand and knelt before him and mocked him, saying, "Hail, King of the Jews!" [30]They spat on him, and took the reed and struck him on the head. [31]After mocking him, they stripped him of the robe and put his own clothes on him. They led him away to crucify him.

... [33]And when they came to a place called Golgotha (which means Place of a Skull), [34]they offered him wine to drink, mixed with gall; but when

he tasted it, he would not drink it. ³⁵And when they had crucified him, they divided his clothes among themselves by casting lots; ³⁶then they sat down there and kept watch over him. ³⁷Over his head they put the charge against him, which read, "This is Jesus, the King of the Jews."

³⁸Then two bandits were crucified with him, one on his right hand and one on his left. ³⁹Those who passed by derided him, shaking their heads ⁴⁰and saying, "You who would destroy the temple and build it in three days, save yourself! If you are the Son of God, come down from the cross." ⁴¹In the same way the chief priests also, along with the scribes and elders, were mocking him, saying, ⁴²"He saved others; he cannot save himself. He is the King of Israel; let him come down from the cross now, and we will believe in him. ⁴³He trusts in God; let God deliver him now, if he wants to; for he said, 'I am God's Son.' " ⁴⁴The bandits who were crucified with him also taunted him in the same way.

⁴⁵From noon on, darkness came over the whole land until three in the afternoon. ⁴⁶And about three o'clock Jesus cried with a loud voice, "Eli, Eli, lema sabachthani?" that is, "My God, my God, why have you forsaken me?" ... ⁵⁰Then Jesus cried again with a loud voice and breathed his last. ... ⁵⁴Now when the centurion and those with him, who were keeping watch over Jesus, saw the earthquake and what took place, they were terrified and said, "Truly this man was God's Son!"

Matthew 27:11–18,20–23,26–31,33–46,50,54
(full lectionary reference: Matthew 27:11–54)

INTRODUCTION

We live in a world that does not always seem to understand faithfulness. "If it's to your benefit, stick to your commitments, but if it's not, go your own way." If marriage causes too much pain, walk away! As soon as you find a company that will give you a little more than your present company, move on! If your church is ensuring trouble, check out that church around the corner that seems to be booming. But what we forget is how important faithfulness is to ensuring a society that is worthwhile to live in. Faithfulness means you can rely on those around you. It means security. Christ didn't take a walk when things got tough. Where would it have left us if he had? He stuck out his commitment to us, through rejection, ridicule and death itself. And because he did, eternity has been opened to us.

NOTES ON THE TEXT

27:11 *Are you the King of the Jews?* That Jesus claimed this title is undoubtedly the charge the Sanhedrin brought before Pilate. By so doing, they made Jesus seem guilty of treason against the kingship of Caesar. Jesus' answer is somewhat evasive, leaving Pilate unsure of how to interpret it.

27:12–14 Rather than wasting his breath trying to defend himself against trumped up charges, Jesus remains silent. He also thereby fulfills the prophecy of Isaiah which Christians related to the Messiah: "... like a sheep that before its shearers is silent, so he did not open his mouth" (Isa. 53:7c).

27:15–22. This custom of releasing a condemned prisoner at Passover is unknown outside of the Gospels. It may have been done in an attempt to placate the Jews during a time of heightened nationalistic fervor.

PERSONAL
QUESTION

27:16 *Jesus Barabbas.* The contrast between these two persons, both named Jesus (which means "God is salvation") is important. One sought to save the nation through military revolution; the other sought to save the world through God's forgiveness and Lordship.

27:46 *"Eli, Eli ..."* This cry is a quote in Aramaic from Psalm 22:1. By echoing this cry, Jesus is identified both with the suffering of the psalmist, and with the triumph of the sufferer, as he ultimately experiences God's deliverance (Psalm 22:19–31).

When has there been a time when your own faithfulness to God and what God was calling you to do has really been tried? How did you respond?

STORY

Corrie ten Boom Identifies With Christ. Corrie ten Boom and her family helped shelter Jews from the Nazis in the Holland of World War II, and for that faithfulness they were sent to concentration camps. For Corrie and her sister Betsie, those camps were also a test of faithfulness, but in that test Christ served as an important example to them. Corrie tells about it in her autobiographical book, *The Hiding Place:*

"Sometimes I would slip the Bible from its little sack with hands that shook, so mysterious had it become to me. It was new; it had just been written. I marveled sometimes that the ink was dry. I had believed the Bible always, but reading it now had nothing to do with belief. It was simply a description of the way things were—of hell and heaven, of how men act and of how God acts. I had read a thousand times the story of Jesus' arrest—how soldiers had slapped Him, laughed at Him, flogged Him. Now such happenings had faces and voices.

"Fridays—the recurrent humiliation of medical inspection. The hospital corridor in which we waited was unheated, and a fall chill had settled into the walls. Still we were forbidden even to wrap ourselves in our own arms, but had to maintain our erect, hands-at-sides position as we filed slowly past a phalanx of grinning guards. How there could have been any pleasure in the sight of these stick-thin legs and hunger-bloated stomachs I could not imagine. Surely there is no more wretched sight than the human body unloved and uncared for. ...

"But it was one of these mornings while we were waiting, shivering in the corridor, that yet another page in the Bible leapt into life for me.

"He hung naked on the cross.

"I had not known—I had not thought. ...The paintings, the carved crucifixes showed at the least a scrap of cloth. But this, I suddenly knew, was the respect and reverence of the artist. But oh—at the time itself, on that other Friday morning—there had been no reverence. No more than I saw in the faces around us now.

"I leaned toward Betsie, ahead of me in line. Her shoulder blades stood out sharp and thin beneath her blue-mottled skin.

" 'Betsie, they took His clothes too.'

"Ahead of me I heard a little gasp. 'Oh, Corrie. And I never thanked Him ...' "[1]

[1]Corrie ten Boom, *The Hiding Place* (Minneapolis, MN: World Wide Publications, 1971), pp. 196–197.

SPRING SEASON
EASTER

Theme: "With Eyes Wide Open"

WEEK 1: EASTER 1

Opening Our Eyes to Hope
John 20:1–18

GATHERING 10 min.	STUDY 30 min.	CARING 20–40 min.

Leader: The agenda has three parts. In the Gathering time you'll be getting to know each other through an "ice-breaker." This will be for your total group. The Study time has two parts: (1) Story and (2) Scripture. If you are short of time, skip the Story and move to the Scripture. Begin by reading out loud the Story or the Scripture to the whole group. Then divide into groups of 4 for the Study time. Finally, regather the total group for the Caring time. Keep to this agenda: (1) Gathering—10 minutes, (2) Study—30 minutes, and (3) Caring—20–40 minutes.

 **Making 'Em Smile.** Go around on question #1 and let everyone share. Then go around again on question #2.

1. When you were in grade school, which of the following would you most likely do if you wanted to make your mother (or primary caregiver) smile?
    - ❐ bring her a picture I made
    - ❐ tell her a "knock knock" joke
    - ❐ tell her I loved her
    - ❐ clean up my room or do a chore
    - ❐ stay out of her way
    - ❐ tell her how pretty she looked

2. Who really made you smile when you were in grade school? What did they do to make you smile?

Opening Our Eyes to Hope
Easter 1 - John 20:1–18

PURPOSE

To see that in a world too often full of despair there are reasons for hope, if we just open our eyes to them.

FOR THE PASTOR

The following material you can use as input for your sermon preparation on this week's Gospel Scripture from the book of John. For further input you may want to share and further comment on the story of Corrie ten Boom, which your study group(s) will be responding to during their session. Also, it's important to share in your sermon or homily your own response to the personal question (or other personally-oriented question) to model personal sharing for your congregation.

SCRIPTURE

20 *Early on the first day of the week, while it was still dark, Mary Magdalene came to the tomb and saw that the stone had been removed from the tomb. ²So she ran and went to Simon Peter and the other disciple, the one whom Jesus loved, and said to them, "They have taken the Lord out of the tomb, and we do not know where they have laid him." ³Then Peter and the other disciple set out and went toward the tomb. ⁴The two were running together, but the other disciple outran Peter and reached the tomb first. ⁵He bent down to look in and saw the linen wrappings lying there, but he did not go in. ⁶Then Simon Peter came, following him, and went into the tomb. He saw the linen wrappings lying there, ⁷and the cloth that had been on Jesus' head, not lying with the linen wrappings but rolled up in a place by itself. ⁸Then the other disciple, who reached the tomb first, also went in, and he saw and believed; ⁹for as yet they did not understand the scripture, that he must rise from the dead. ¹⁰Then the disciples returned to their homes.*

¹¹But Mary stood weeping outside the tomb. As she wept, she bent over to look into the tomb; ¹²and she saw two angels in white, sitting where the body of Jesus had been lying, one at the head and the other at the feet. ¹³They said to her, "Woman, why are you weeping?" She said to them, "They have taken away my Lord, and I do not know where they have laid him." ¹⁴When she had said this, she turned around and saw Jesus standing there, but she did not know that it was Jesus. ¹⁵Jesus said to her, "Woman, why are you weeping? Whom are you looking for?" Supposing him to be the gardener, she said to him, "Sir, if you have carried him away, tell me where you have laid him, and I will take him away." ¹⁶Jesus said to her, "Mary!" She turned and said to him in Hebrew, "Rabbouni!" (which means Teacher). ¹⁷Jesus said to her, "Do not hold on to me, because I have not yet ascended to the Father. But go to my brothers and say to them, 'I am

INTRODUCTION

Hoping is hard work. It is hard work because if those hopes are dashed, one loses a lot of emotional energy. There are many people in our society who seem to have lost the energy required to hope—those who have been "burned" many times in abusive relationships; people who have lost a loved one who was very close to them, and cannot seem to reinvest in someone else for fear they might lose that person too; those who have tried many different life philosophies and have found them empty. Many such people are like an experiment that has been done with two rats: if you hold one rat in your hand firmly so that no matter how valiantly he struggles he cannot escape, he will finally give up. Then if you throw that rat into a tank of warm water, he will sink, not swim. He has "learned" to give up, that there is no point in struggling. But if you throw another rat into the same water, one that doesn't "know" that his situation is hopeless, the rat will swim to safety. Many people are drowning in despair when they have the power to swim to safety. Jesus' resurrection helps us to see that all is not hopeless—that there is safety in the arms of the God who controls life and death. As that hope revived the first disciples, it can revive us, too.

NOTES ON THE TEXT

20:1 *while it was still dark.* This probably has both literal and figurative significance. The other Gospels mention that it was very early, but this author's intent is to emphasize that spiritually it was still dark—for it seemed the darkness had overcome the light since the Resurrection was not yet known (see 1:5; 9:4). ***Mary Magdalene.*** Mary is mentioned in all four Gospel accounts of the Resurrection. Magdala was a village in Galilee near Capernaum. Luke 8:2 says she was one of several women who traveled with the disciples. The other Gospels mention Mary was accompanied by other women, but this author's focus is only on her. ***stone.*** The tomb was in a cave, the entrance of which was sealed by a large stone.

20:2 *the one whom Jesus loved.* This refers to John, the author of this Gospel. It is not being claimed here that John was the only disciple whom Jesus loved, only that he felt a special relationship with Jesus. ***They have taken the Lord.*** Mary seems to have assumed that since Jesus was laid in the tomb of a rich man (see John 19:38–41), grave robbers had plundered it, hoping to find wealth buried there as well. ***we do not know.*** Just as the other Gospels record, this indicates that Mary did not go to the tomb alone.

20:5–7 *saw the linen wrappings.* Why the "other disciple" hesitated to go in until after Peter did is unknown. The author describes the arrangement of the clothes, the sight of which inspired faith at least in the "other disciple," at some length. Grave robbers, in search of treasures entombed with the corpse, would either have taken the body still wrapped up, or scattered the strips as they tore them off. The fact that the clothes were neatly laid by was one of the evidences that led the disciples to faith.

PERSONAL QUESTION

When did you feel yourself to be "utterly and unarguably defeated"? What, if anything, brought you hope?

STORY

Corrie ten Boom Finds Hope in Isolation. Corrie ten Boom and her family sheltered Jews from the Nazis during World War II. Eventually, however, she was caught and was sent to one of the infamous Nazi concentration camps. One time when she was ill she was thrown into an isolation cell. Even there, however, she found a message of hope from God. She tells of this in her book, *The Hiding Place:*

"In only one way was this new cell an improvement over the first one. It had a window. Seven iron bars ran across it, four bars up and down. It was high in the wall, much too high to look out of, but through those twenty-eight squares I could see the sky.

"All day I kept my eyes fixed on that bit of heaven. Sometimes clouds moved across the squares, white or pink or edged with gold, and when the wind was from the west I could hear the sea. Best of all, for nearly an hour each day, gradually lengthening as the spring sun rose higher, a shaft of checkered light streamed into the dark little room. As the weather turned warmer and I grew stronger I would stand up to catch the sunshine on my face and chest, moving along the wall with the moving light, climbing at last onto the cot to stand on tiptoe in the final rays.

"As my health returned, I was able to use my eyes longer. I had been sustaining myself from my Scriptures a verse at a time, now like a starving man I gulped entire Gospels at a reading, seeing whole the magnificent drama of salvation.

"And as I did, an incredible thought pricked the back of my neck. Was it possible that this—all of this that seemed so wasteful and so needless—this war, Scheveningen prison, this very cell, none of it was unforeseen or accidental? Could it be part of the pattern first revealed in the Gospels? Hadn't Jesus—and here my reading became intent indeed—hadn't Jesus been defeated as utterly and unarguably as our little group and our small plans had been?

"But ... if the Gospels were truly the pattern of God's activity, then defeat was only the beginning. I would look around at the bare little cell and wonder what conceivable victory could come from a place like this."[1]

[1]Corrie ten Boom, *The Hiding Place* (Minneapolis, MN: World Wide Publications, 1971), p. 157.

Small Group
HANDOUT

WEEK 2: EASTER 2

Opening Our Eyes to Faith
John 20:19–31

 **GATHERING**
10 min.

 **STUDY**
30 min.

 **CARING**
20–40 min.

Leader: The agenda has three parts. In the Gathering time you'll be getting to know each other through an "ice-breaker." This will be for your total group. The Study time has two parts: (1) Story and (2) Scripture. If you are short of time, skip the Story and move to the Scripture. Begin by reading out loud the Story or the Scripture to the whole group. Then divide into groups of 4 for the Study time. Finally, regather the total group for the Caring time. Keep to this agenda: (1) Gathering—10 minutes, (2) Study—30 minutes, and (3) Caring—20–40 minutes.

 **Just My Style.** Go around on #1, letting everyone share their answer, and then do the same with #2.

1. When it comes to fashion, I'm the kind of person who ...
   - ❒ thinks "formal dress" means my jeans without the holes in them.
   - ❒ wears what I like, whether it's in fashion or not.
   - ❒ insists on designer labels—even on my underwear!
   - ❒ keeps with the fashion, as best as I can afford to.
   - ❒ tries to set fashion trends myself.

2. When you talk about eating out, my style is more like ...
   - ❒ McDonald's or Burger King.
   - ❒ anywhere with good pizza.
   - ❒ a good steak house.
   - ❒ a fine seafood restaurant by the ocean.
   - ❒ Mexican food that brings the steam out my ears.
   - ❒ a restaurant with exotic cuisine at the top of a skyscraper.
   - ❒ a health food restaurant with creative recipes.

Opening Our Eyes to Faith
Easter 2 - John 20:19–31

PURPOSE

To consider what it means to open our sometimes cynical eyes to the experience of faith.

FOR THE PASTOR

The following material you can use as input for your sermon preparation on this week's Gospel Scripture from the book of John. For further input you may want to share and further comment on the story of C.S. Lewis., which your study group(s) will be responding to during their session. Also, it's important to share in your sermon or homily your own response to the personal question (or other personally-oriented question) to model personal sharing for your congregation.

SCRIPTURE

[19]When it was evening on that day, the first day of the week, and the doors of the house where the disciples had met were locked for fear of the Jews, Jesus came and stood among them and said, "Peace be with you." [20]After he said this, he showed them his hands and his side. Then the disciples rejoiced when they saw the Lord. [21]Jesus said to them again, "Peace be with you. As the Father has sent me, so I send you." [22]When he had said this, he breathed on them and said to them, "Receive the Holy Spirit. [23]If you forgive the sins of any, they are forgiven them; if you retain the sins of any, they are retained."

[24]But Thomas (who was called the Twin), one of the twelve, was not with them when Jesus came. [25]So the other disciples told him, "We have seen the Lord." But he said to them, "Unless I see the mark of the nails in his hands, and put my finger in the mark of the nails and my hand in his side, I will not believe."

[26]A week later his disciples were again in the house, and Thomas was with them. Although the doors were shut, Jesus came and stood among them and said, "Peace be with you." [27]Then he said to Thomas, "Put your finger here and see my hands. Reach out your hand and put it in my side. Do not doubt but believe." [28]Thomas answered him, "My Lord and my God!" [29]Jesus said to him, "Have you believed because you have seen me? Blessed are those who have not seen and yet have come to believe."

[30]Now Jesus did many other signs in the presence of his disciples, which are not written in this book. [31]But these are written so that you may come to believe that Jesus is the Messiah, the Son of God, and that through believing you may have life in his name.

John 20:19–31

Seeing with the eyes of faith is an essential skill for living. Without that skill, one cannot have close relationships. How do we know a person is trustworthy and likely to show us love and friendship in a reliable way? We cannot see inside their heart. Whatever visible or tangible evidences they can give us of their intent can as easily be carefully contrived manipulations. But at some point with each close relationship we develop, we have to be able to say, "I'm going to look with the eyes of faith beyond what I can see, and trust this person." We also cannot see our own future. How do we know that whatever is there in our future is worth what we must sacrifice now? We don't! But building a promising future requires that we have enough faith in the future to make the sacrifices. Building a strong spiritual life also requires this skill. We need to believe in a God we cannot see, who holds out promises we often cannot receive until we reach out to accept them. It is only when we have such eyes of faith that we truly learn what life can be.

20:19 *fear of the Jews.* When this Gospel says "Jews" it generally means "Jewish authorities." The disciples themselves were Jews, as was Jesus. In spite of Jesus' words in John 14:27, the disciples were afraid that the authorities, who had been successful in having Jesus killed, might now turn their anti-insurrection argument against them. ***Jesus came.*** Nothing is said about how Jesus came to be among them, but the implication of the locked doors appears to be that Jesus simply materialized in the room (see also verse 26 and Paul's discussion of the resurrection body in 1 Cor. 15:35–49).

20:22 *he breathed on them.* As God originally breathed the breath of life into Adam at the first creation (Gen. 2:7), so now Jesus breathes the breath of spiritual life into his people at this, the re-creation of the people of God. ***Receive the Holy Spirit.*** The word for "spirit" and "breath" is the same word in Greek (*pneuma*) as well as in Hebrew (*rhuah*).

20:25 *Unless I see.* According to Luke 24:38, all the apostles experienced doubt. Here also it should be noted that Thomas was asking for no more evidence than what Jesus had already given the others (see v. 20). Perhaps Thomas was the one in the group who asked the questions which others were thinking. His other actions, as recorded in this Gospel, show him as a courageous skeptic who gave voice to his questions (see 11:16 and 14:5).

20:29 *Blessed are those.* While questioning is natural and necessary, Jesus her blesses those throughout time who would believe without having to see.

20:30–31 These words, which may have been an original ending of the Gospel, speak of the "editorial policy" with which the author chose his material, and the purpose for which he wrote.

C.S. Lewis speaks of some adults who "are forgetting what boyhood felt like from within." What do you remember your boyhood or girlhood "feeling like from within"? Do you think your experiences made you more, or less, receptive to faith?

C.S. Lewis' Childhood Pessimism. C.S. Lewis has become one of the Christian faith's most popular writers. But for Lewis' early life, he was not a Christian at all. In the book he wrote about his conversion, *Surprised by Joy,* he tells of his childhood pessimism that remained with him well into adulthood:

"In addition to this, and equally working against my faith, there was in me a deeply ingrained pessimism; a pessimism, by that time, much more of intellect than of temper. I was now by no means unhappy; but I had very definitely formed the opinion that the universe was, in the main, a rather regrettable institution. I am well aware that some will feel disgust and some will laugh, at the idea of a loutish, well-fed boy in an Eton collar, passing an unfavorable judgment on the cosmos. ... They are forgetting what boyhood felt like from within. ... As to the sources of my pessimism, the reader will remember that, though in many ways most fortunate, yet I had very early in life met a great dismay. But I am now inclined to think that the seeds of pessimism were sown before my mother's death. Ridiculous as it may sound, I believe that the clumsiness of my hands was at the root of the matter. How could this be? Not, certainly, that a child says, 'I can't cut a straight line with a pair of scissors, therefore the universe is evil.' Childhood has no such power of generalization and is not (to do it justice) so silly. Nor did my clumsiness produce what is ordinarily called an Inferiority Complex. I was not comparing myself to other boys; my defeats occurred in solitude. What they really bred in me was a deep (and, of course, inarticulate) sense of resistance or opposition on the part of inanimate things. Even that makes it too abstract and adult. Perhaps I had better call it a settled expectation that everything would do what you did not want it to do. Whatever you wanted to remain straight, would bend; whatever you tried to bend would fly back to the straight; all knots which you wished to be firm would come untied; all knots you wanted to untie would remain firm. It is not possible to put it into language without making it comic. ... But it is perhaps just these early experiences which are so fugitive and, to an adult, so grotesque, that give the mind its earliest bias, its habitual sense of what is or is not plausible."[1]

Small Group
HANDOUT

WEEK 3: EASTER 3

Opening Our Eyes to His Presence

Luke 24:13–35

 **GATHERING**
10 min.

 **STUDY**
30 min.

 **CARING**
20–40 min.

Leader: The agenda has three parts. In the Gathering time you'll be getting to know each other through an "ice-breaker." This will be for your total group. The Study time has two parts: (1) Story and (2) Scripture. If you are short of time, skip the Story and move to the Scripture. Begin by reading out loud the Story or the Scripture to the whole group. Then divide into groups of 4 for the Study time. Finally, regather the total group for the Caring time. Keep to this agenda: (1) Gathering—10 minutes, (2) Study—30 minutes, and (3) Caring—20–40 minutes.

 **Myself as an Appliance.** Go around on question #1 and let everyone share. Then go around again on question #2.

1. If you could compare the role you have taken in your family down through time to a household appliance, what appliance would it be?

    ❒ vacuum cleaner—I pick up after everyone.

    ❒ washing machine agitator—When things get too calm I stir things up!

    ❒ heater—When people come in from the cold, difficult world I warm them up!

    ❒ television—I'm the entertainer.

    ❒ smoke alarm—I keep others alert to dangers.

    ❒ thermostat—I keep things comfortable.

    ❒ refrigerator—I provide all of the good stuff people seem to want.

    ❒ electric screwdriver—I fix things and keep them running.

2. How happy are you with this role right now?

Opening Our Eyes to His Presence
Easter 3 - Luke 24:13–35

PURPOSE

To understand how God is always present and acting around us, if we only open our eyes to his presence.

FOR THE PASTOR

The following material you can use as input for your sermon preparation on this week's Gospel Scripture from the book of Luke. For further input you may want to share and further comment on the story of John Wesley, which your study group(s) will be responding to during their session. Also, it's important to share in your sermon or homily your own response to the personal question (or other personally-oriented question) to model personal sharing for your congregation.

SCRIPTURE

[13]Now on that same day two of them were going to a village called Emmaus, about seven miles from Jerusalem, [14]and talking with each other about all these things that had happened. [15]While they were talking and discussing, Jesus himself came near and went with them, [16]but their eyes were kept from recognizing him. [17]And he said to them, "What are you discussing with each other while you walk along?" They stood still, looking sad. [18]Then one of them, whose name was Cleopas, answered him, "Are you the only stranger in Jerusalem who does not know the things that have taken place there in these days?" [19]He asked them, "What things?" They replied, "The things about Jesus of Nazareth, who was a prophet mighty in deed and word before God and all the people, [20]and how our chief priests and leaders handed him over to be condemned to death and crucified him. [21]But we had hoped that he was the one to redeem Israel. Yes, and besides all this, it is now the third day since these things took place. [22]Moreover, some women of our group astounded us. They were at the tomb early this morning, [23]and when they did not find his body there, they came back and told us that they had indeed seen a vision of angels who said that he was alive. [24]Some of those who were with us went to the tomb and found it just as the women had said; but they did not see him." [25]Then he said to them, "Oh, how foolish you are, and how slow of heart to believe all that the prophets have declared! [26]Was it not necessary that the Messiah should suffer these things and then enter into his glory?" [27]Then beginning with Moses and all the prophets, he interpreted to them the things about himself in all the scriptures.

[28]As they came near the village to which they were going, he walked ahead as if he were going on. [29]But they urged him strongly, saying, "Stay with us, because it is almost evening and the day is now nearly over." So he went in to stay with them. [30]When he was at the table with them, he took bread, blessed and broke it, and gave it to them. [31]Then their eyes were

opened, and they recognized him; and he vanished from their sight. ³²They said to each other, "Were not our hearts burning within us while he was talking to us on the road, while he was opening the scriptures to us?" ³³That same hour they got up and returned to Jerusalem; and they found the eleven and their companions gathered together. ³⁴They were saying, "The Lord has risen indeed, and he has appeared to Simon!" ³⁵Then they told what had happened on the road, and how he had been made known to them in the breaking of the bread.

Luke 24:13–35

INTRODUCTION

Sometimes people ask the question, "Where is God when I'm hurting?" The implication is that God has somehow abandoned them. But the truth is that God walks with us every step of the way. We, however, do not always recognize his presence. Why *don't* we recognize his presence? Perhaps it is because we have false expectations about what his presence with us means. Perhaps we think that if God were really present with us, nothing bad would happen. But Jesus himself had to face injustice and his eventual crucifixion. Or perhaps we think that if God were really present with us we would have some sort of tingly feeling. But Jesus never promised tingly feelings: he just promised to be with us always "to the end of the age" (Matt. 28:20). Perhaps we think that if God were really with us we would see some kind of supernatural manifestation. But looking for him in that way makes us miss him as he walks beside us in the normal day-to-day activities of life. Ultimately, we need to accept in faith that Jesus is walking beside us. When we do that we gain an inner peace from knowing that we can turn to him at any time and in any place for comfort and support.

NOTES ON THE TEXT

21:13 *Emmaus.* It is uncertain where this town was, but two main possibilities exist, both of which were relatively near to Jerusalem. The Jewish historian Josephus speaks of an "Emmaus" about four miles from Jerusalem that was chosen by Vespasian as the site for a colony of Roman soldiers after A.D. 70. In Maccabean times another town, about 15 miles from Jerusalem on the Jaffa road, was known as Emmaus.

24:25 *slow of heart.* They may have believed in their head, but not in their heart. The message was slow to reach them at the level of their deepest feeling.

24:26 *necessary that the Messiah should suffer.* Isaiah 53 showed the importance of the Messiah suffering.

24:29 *Stay with us ...* These two disciples were apparently returning to their home in Emmaus. The fact that the day was nearly almost over would mean that it would be getting dark, and not safe to travel alone. Hospitality to fellow travelers was considered an important social duty.

24:30 *he took bread, blessed and broke it ...* While this is a simple enough description of how a meal would begin, it is probably meant to carry overtones of the Lord's Supper. By participating in this with faith, Luke's readers likewise would have their eyes opened to recognize Jesus as the Lord.

24:32 *Were not our hearts burning within us ...?* Both the Psalmist (Psalm 39:3) and Jeremiah (Jeremiah 20:9) used this metaphor of a sense of fire or burning in the heart. In both cases it seems to refer to the Word of God within that must be expressed.

If you were to pick someone to go with you for a long walk on a country road, who would you pick and why?

John Wesley's "Heartburn." John Wesley was the founding father of the Methodists and the Wesleyan traditions, as well as an influential force in the "Great Awakening" that swept America in the 18th century. But throughout much of Wesley's early ministry, he preached and taught while having a great spiritual void in his own heart. One day, however, he had an experience which he described as nothing less than a "conversion" on Aldersgate Street in London. The story is told in John Pudney's, *John Wesley and His World:*

"So Wesley, while still seeking the experience of vital faith for himself, now began to preach the gospel of justification by faith alone. ...

"May 24 was the culminating point in that significant month, and it is best described in Wesley's own words: 'I think it was about five this morning, that I opened my Testament on those words ...' There are given unto us exceeding great and precious promises, even that ye should be partakers of the divine nature." Just as I went out, I opened it again on those words, "Thou art not far from the kingdom of God." In the afternoon I was asked to go to St. Paul's. The anthem was "Out of the deep have I called unto Thee, O Lord: Lord, hear my voice." ...

" 'In the evening I went very unwillingly to a society in Aldersgate Street, where one was reading Luther's preface to the Epistle of Romans. About a quarter before nine, while he was describing the change which God works in the heart through faith in Christ, I felt my heart strangely warmed. I felt I did trust in Christ, Christ alone for my salvation; and an assurance was given me that He had taken away my sins, even mine, and saved me from the law of sin and death.

" 'I began to pray with all my might for those who had in a more especial manner despitefully used me and persecuted me. I then testified openly to all there what I now first felt in my heart. But it was not long before the enemy suggested, "This cannot be faith; for where is thy joy?" Then was I taught that peace and victory over sin are essential to faith in the Captain of our salvation; but that, as to the transports of joy that usually attend the beginning of it, especially in those who have mourned deeply, God sometimes giveth, sometimes withholdeth them, according to the counsels of His own will.' "[1]

[1] John Pudney, *John Wesley and His World* (London, England: Thames & Hudson, 1978), pp. 56–57.

SERENDIPITY

Small Group

H A N D O U T

WEEK 4: EASTER 4

Opening Our Eyes to Security

John 10:1–10

 **GATHERING**
10 min.

 **STUDY**
30 min.

 **CARING**
20–40 min.

Leader: The agenda has three parts. In the Gathering time you'll be getting to know each other through an "ice-breaker." This will be for your total group. The Study time has two parts: (1) Story and (2) Scripture. If you are short of time, skip the Story and move to the Scripture. Begin by reading out loud the Story or the Scripture to the whole group. Then divide into groups of 4 for the Study time. Finally, regather the total group for the Caring time. Keep to this agenda: (1) Gathering—10 minutes, (2) Study—30 minutes, and (3) Caring—20–40 minutes.

 **My Favorite Things.** In *The Sound of Music*, Maria says that when sad or painful events happen to her, she "simply remembers my favorite things, and then I don't feel so bad." Take some time now to think about and share those favorite things.

1. When you were between 6 and 10 years old, which of the following would you have included as part of your "favorite things"?

   ❏ a day off from school ❏ my pet
   ❏ having a sleep-over with my friends ❏ Christmas
   ❏ watching television ❏ stuffed animals
   ❏ sports ❏ reading
   ❏ going to my grandparents' house ❏ other:___________

2. What do you count as your "favorite things" now?

   ❏ hiking and camping ❏ sports (still!)
   ❏ listening to music ❏ Christmas (still!)
   ❏ exercising ❏ traveling
   ❏ spending time with my family ❏ gardening
   ❏ having time to myself ❏ reading
   ❏ relaxing with friends ❏ other:___________

<table>
<tr><td>SESSION

4</td><td><h1>Opening Our Eyes to Security</h1>
Easter 4 - John 10:1–10</td></tr>
</table>

PURPOSE

To be able to more clearly see how turning our life over to Jesus Christ gives us a greater security because of his loving care for us.

FOR THE PASTOR

The following material you can use as input for your sermon preparation on this week's Gospel Scripture from the book of John. For further input you may want to share and further comment on the story of Desmond Tutu, which your study group(s) will be responding to during their session. Also, it's important to share in your sermon or homily your own response to the personal question (or other personally-oriented question) to model personal sharing for your congregation.

SCRIPTURE

10 *"Very truly, I tell you, anyone who does not enter the sheepfold by the gate but climbs in by another way is a thief and a bandit. [2]The one who enters by the gate is the shepherd of the sheep. [3]The gatekeeper opens the gate for him, and the sheep hear his voice. He calls his own sheep by name and leads them out. [4]When he has brought out all his own, he goes ahead of them, and the sheep follow him because they know his voice. [5]They will not follow a stranger, but they will run from him because they do not know the voice of strangers." [6]Jesus used this figure of speech with them, but they did not understand what he was saying to them.*

[7]So again Jesus said to them, "Very truly, I tell you, I am the gate for the sheep. [8]All who came before me are thieves and bandits; but the sheep did not listen to them. [9]I am the gate. Whoever enters by me will be saved, and will come in and go out and find pasture. [10]The thief comes only to steal and kill and destroy. I came that they may have life, and have it abundantly.

John 10:1–10

INTRODUCTION

Anyone who has ever had a young dog knows there are times that you can call that dog to safety—the safety of indoors or a fenced-in backyard—and the dog will flee that safety for a dangerous street. In time the dog learns that there is security in the protective guidance of its owners. Human beings are like that, too. We want our freedom to go our own way, but then we learn that without guidance we get ourselves into trouble. Christ gives us our freedom, but as the Good Shepherd he also seeks to give us firm guidance away from those behaviors and situations where we might find ourselves in spiritual danger. This function of guidance he also gives to the pastoral leadership of our churches who seek to give protective guidance to the "sheep" under their care.

10:1 *sheepfold.* Sheep were herded into stone wall enclosures at night as a protection against predators and thieves.

10:3 *The gatekeeper.* Although both the shepherd and the gate clearly represent Jesus (vv. 7,9), the figure of the gatekeeper is not explained. In a parable, unlike an allegory, not all the details have a meaning. *calls his own sheep by name.* Shepherds had names and calls for their sheep as a means of aiding them in separating their flocks from mixed herds such as would be found in a typical sheep pen.

10:4 *he goes ahead of them.* Note that the shepherd here does not drive the sheep from behind, but leads them by going ahead of them. Thus, that the sheep go forward is not because they fear what is behind, but because they are drawn in trust by the shepherd who goes ahead of them. That is the way Jesus leads his "sheep."

10:7 *I am the gate.* This symbol is stated forthrightly in 14:6 where Jesus says he is the way to God.

10:8 *thieves and bandits.* In this context Jesus is referring, not to Moses and the other legitimate leaders before him, but to the so-called religious leaders who exploited the people for their own ends (2:14–15; see Ezekiel 34:1–6).

10:10 *have it abundantly.* The Old Testament anticipated that the Messiah would bring fullness and plenty to the land (Amos 9:13). Jesus' affirmation of this in a spiritual context is another indicator of his identity.

Who has been a "good shepherd" to you in your life?

Desmond Tutu Becomes a Pastor. Many people throughout the world know Desmond Tutu as an influential political figure who helped overturn apartheid in his native country of South Africa. But before he was a political figure, he was a Bishop and before he was a Bishop he was a pastor, and before he was a pastor he was a school teacher. When he became a priest and pastor (the word "pastor" is derived from shepherding), he discovered something of what it meant to care for people. We read of his experience in Shirley DuBoulay's book, *Tutu: Voice of the Voiceless:*

"He also discovered the privilege of priesthood. 'There is the joy of being welcomed into a home as you go around visiting the parishioners. And people share some of their deepest secrets with you; that always leaves me feeling very humble.' His easy, loving way with people endeared him to the parishioners, who were so fond of him that it has even been suggested that Canon Mokoatla was a bit jealous. Tutu, in turn, was deeply impressed by the people he met, 'staggered at the strength of their attachment to Our Lord and amazed by the strange kind of joy they have in the midst of their poverty and suffering. They sometimes brought tears to my eyes. I was infinitely more well off than they were, but when I was grousing they were able to thank God for something good that had happened to them.'

"Years later Desmond spoke of pastoral visiting to a group of Deacons about to be ordained as priests: 'You can sit all day in your house and not visit your people, not take communion to the sick, the aged and nobody will usually complain to you, but your church will grow emptier. You can't love people and not visit them. You can't love them unless you know them, and you can't know them unless you visit them regularly. A good shepherd knows his sheep by name.'

"Tutu was becoming a pastor, the best sort of pastor who cares, really cares, about his parishioners."[1]

---

[1]Shirley DuBoulay, *Tutu: Voice of the Voiceless* (London, England: Hodder & Stoughton Publishers, 1988), p. 56.

WEEK 5: EASTER 5
Opening Our Eyes to the Way
John 14:1–14

 **GATHERING**
10 min.

 **STUDY**
30 min.

 **CARING**
20–40 min.

Leader: The agenda has three parts. In the Gathering time you'll be getting to know each other through an "ice-breaker." This will be for your total group. The Study time has two parts: (1) Story and (2) Scripture. If you are short of time, skip the Story and move to the Scripture. Begin by reading out loud the Story or the Scripture to the whole group. Then divide into groups of 4 for the Study time. Finally, regather the total group for the Caring time. Keep to this agenda: (1) Gathering—10 minutes, (2) Study—30 minutes, and (3) Caring—20–40 minutes.

 **Color My World.** Choose a color that best expresses how things are going in each of the following parts of your world:

COLORS:

Green—full of life	Yellow—warm and vibrant
Orange—full of conflict and tension	Brown—dull and ordinary
Blue—cold	Gray—gloomy
Purple—richly unique	

MY WORK WORLD: _____________

MY HOME LIFE: _______________

MY FRIENDSHIPS: ____________

MY LEISURE WORLD: _________

MY LOVE LIFE: ________________

MY SPIRITUAL LIFE:____________

Opening Our Eyes to the Way
Easter 5 - John 14:1–14

PURPOSE

To be able to get past the confusion of competing directions in this world in order to discover how Christ shows us a better way.

FOR THE PASTOR

The following material you can use as input for your sermon preparation on this week's Gospel Scripture from the book of John. For further input you may want to share and further comment on the story of Thomas Merton, which your study group(s) will be responding to during their session. Also, it's important to share in your sermon or homily your own response to the personal question (or other personally-oriented question) to model personal sharing for your congregation.

SCRIPTURE

14 *"Do not let your hearts be troubled. Believe in God, believe also in me. [2]In my Father's house there are many dwelling places. If it were not so, would I have told you that I go to prepare a place for you? [3]And if I go and prepare a place for you, I will come again and will take you to myself, so that where I am, there you may be also. [4]And you know the way to the place where I am going." [5]Thomas said to him, "Lord, we do not know where you are going. How can we know the way?" [6]Jesus said to him, "I am the way, and the truth, and the life. No one comes to the Father except through me. [7]If you know me, you will know my Father also. From now on you do know him and have seen him."*

[8]Philip said to him, "Lord, show us the Father, and we will be satisfied." [9]Jesus said to him, "Have I been with you all this time, Philip, and you still do not know me? Whoever has seen me has seen the Father. How can you say, 'Show us the Father'? [10]Do you not believe that I am in the Father and the Father is in me? The words that I say to you I do not speak on my own; but the Father who dwells in me does his works. [11]Believe me that I am in the Father and the Father is in me; but if you do not, then believe me because of the works themselves. [12]Very truly, I tell you, the one who believes in me will also do the works that I do and, in fact, will do greater works than these, because I am going to the Father. [13]I will do whatever you ask in my name, so that the Father may be glorified in the Son. [14]If in my name you ask me for anything, I will do it."

John 14:1–14

INTRODUCTION

Michael W. Smith sang a popular song a few years ago called "A Place in This World." The song appeals to young people who wonder if they really belong. Many of us at various times feel like we don't have a place—like we don't belong anywhere. Our Scripture for this week asserts that this will not be the case in eternal life. Jesus went to prepare a place for us, a unique place suited to our uniqueness. He also prepared our way. He did so by dying on the cross for our sins, and then going to the right hand of the Father to be our advocate. No other religious figure even begins to claim so much.

14:1 *... believe also in me.* Belief in Christ is presented as a corollary to belief in God, which most of his hearers would already profess.

14:2 *many dwelling places.* The emphasis is on the fact that there is room for all in heaven. That he is going to prepare a place adds a personalized aspect to heaven—a unique place is prepared for each person. It is like your room is personally prepared for you when you get to the "bed and breakfast."

14:8–9 *show us the Father.* John has already said, "No one has ever seen God. It is God the only Son ... who has made him known" (1:18). Jesus continues that theme by saying, "Whoever has seen me has seen the Father."

14:12 *greater works than these.* This is not because the disciples are greater or are more powerful than Christ, but because the same Father who works in him will work through the disciples (v. 10b), and he will build on what he did in Christ, making it even greater.

14:13–14 Jesus is not intending to be understood as a genie. Prayer must be asked "in his name" (v. 13), that is, in accord with his character and purpose of bringing glory to the Father. This promise assumes believers are submitting to the will of the Father just as Jesus did. In that case, they can have the same assurance Jesus did that the Father will hear them.

If you were to design your own special "dwelling place" in heaven, what would you want to make sure it had?

Thomas Merton's Conversion. Thomas Merton was raised in a family where God was relegated to the sidelines of life. But over time he began to experience a void in his life, and he began to show a deep hunger for spiritual direction. He was eventually led to the Catholic Church, where he became a Trappist monk. This conversion came over a period of time, but an important influence was the stress of World War II beginning. He tells the story in *The Seven Storey Mountain:*

"All the internal contradictions of the society in which I lived were at last beginning to converge upon its heart. There could not be much more of a delay in its dismembering. Where would it end? In those days the future was obscured, blanked out by a war as by a dead-end wall. Nobody knew if anyone at all would come out alive. ...

"I knew that I myself hated war, and all the motives that led to war and were behind wars. But I could see that now my likes or dislikes, beliefs or disbeliefs meant absolutely nothing in the external, political order. I was just an individual, and the individual had ceased to count. ...

[He writes of borrowing a book on the life of Gerard Manley Hopkins and walking home.]

"I took up the book about Gerard Manley Hopkins. The chapter told of Hopkins at Balliol, at Oxford. He was thinking of becoming a Catholic. He was writing letters to Cardinal Newman (not yet a cardinal) about becoming a Catholic.

"All of a sudden, something began to stir within me, something began to push me, to prompt me. It was a movement that spoke like a voice.

" 'What are you waiting for?' it said. 'Why are you sitting here? Why do you still hesitate? You know what you ought to do? Why don't you do it?' ...

"Hopkins was writing to Newman, at Birmingham, about his indecision.

" 'What are you waiting for?' said the voice within me again. 'Why are you sitting there? It is useless to hesitate any longer. Why don't you get up and go?'

"I got up and walked restlessly around the room. 'It's absurd,' I thought. 'Anyway, Father Ford would not be there at this time of day. I would only be wasting time.'

"Hopkins had written to Newman, and Newman had replied to him, telling him to come and see him at Birmingham.

"Suddenly, I could bear it no longer. I put down the book, and got into my raincoat, and started down the stairs. I went out into the street. I crossed over, and walked along by the grey wooden fence, towards Broadway, in the light rain.

"And then everything inside me began to sing—to sing with peace, to sing with strength and to sing with conviction."[1]

[1]Thomas Merton, *The Seven Storey Mountain* , pp. 238–239. © Harcourt, Brace & Company. All rights reserved.

Small Group
HANDOUT

WEEK 6: EASTER 6

Opening Our Eyes to the Spirit's Direction

John 14:15–21

 GATHERING
10 min.

 STUDY
30 min.

 CARING
20–40 min.

Leader: The agenda has three parts. In the Gathering time you'll be getting to know each other through an "ice-breaker." This will be for your total group. The Study time has two parts: (1) Story and (2) Scripture. If you are short of time, skip the Story and move to the Scripture. Begin by reading out loud the Story or the Scripture to the whole group. Then divide into groups of 4 for the Study time. Finally, regather the total group for the Caring time. Keep to this agenda: (1) Gathering—10 minutes, (2) Study—30 minutes, and (3) Caring—20–40 minutes.

 **You Remind Me of ...** Write your name on a slip of paper and put it in a hat. Let everyone in the group select a name from the hat. Choose a building that best describes that person. When everyone is finished, read out loud the particular building you selected, and see if the group can guess your selection:

YELLOWSTONE LODGE: You are stately and rustic, a solidly-built place for people to find rest while on their grand adventure.
MAGNIFICENT SKYSCRAPER: You keep us looking upward!
RESORT HOTEL: People come to you to recuperate and to escape the pressures of their lives. You offer hospitality and luxury.
FORT KNOX: You are a strong vault, full of precious treasures.
U.N. BUILDING: People look to you for guidance in conflict.
THE LOUVRE: You are full of creativity and masterpieces. Anyone who sees what you have inside is stunned by the beauty.
ROSE BOWL: You are a place where people go to celebrate and have a good time.
ST. PATRICK'S CATHEDRAL: When people are near you, they sense your spirituality.

Opening Our Eyes to the Spirit's Direction
Easter 6 - John 14:15–21

PURPOSE

To learn how to see more clearly the ways the Holy Spirit guides us.

FOR THE PASTOR

The following material you can use as input for your sermon preparation on this week's Gospel Scripture from the book of John. For further input you may want to share and further comment on the story of Mother Teresa, which your study group(s) will be responding to during their session. Also, it's important to share in your sermon or homily your own response to the personal question (or other personally-oriented question) to model personal sharing for your congregation.

SCRIPTURE

"[15]If you love me, you will keep my commandments. [16]And I will ask the Father, and he will give you another Advocate, to be with you forever. [17]This is the Spirit of truth, whom the world cannot receive, because it neither sees him nor knows him. You know him, because he abides with you, and he will be in you.

[18]"I will not leave you orphaned; I am coming to you. [19]In a little while the world will no longer see me, but you will see me; because I live, you also will live. [20]On that day you will know that I am in my Father, and you in me, and I in you. [21]They who have my commandments and keep them are those who love me; and those who love me will be loved by my Father, and I will love them and reveal myself to them."

John 14:15–21

INTRODUCTION

Albert Einstein is reported to have once said, "Perfection of means and confusion of goals seem—in my opinion—to characterize our age." Certainly his words apply to our day as well. Knowledge and our technical abilities are increasing in exponential terms. Computers put not only entire encyclopedias, but entire libraries, at our fingertips. We have dubbed our era "the information age." But our only problem is that we don't know how we are supposed to use all of that information. Is it solely to make more money? Is it to win out over others (who also have that information at their fingertips)? Unfortunately, the result of all that educated self-focus has been things like insider-trading scandals, new mind-altering drugs, new weapons of destruction, and new tensions between the "haves" and the "have-nots." We are like the joke told about the pilot who came over the P.A. in his commercial airline. He said, "I've got good news and I've got bad news. The bad news is that we are hopelessly lost! The good news, however, is that we are making excellent time!" Only when we let the love of God direct our information-gathering will progress toward a better world, and better lives for all of us, be made.

14:15 *If you love me ...* This establishes the importance of Jesus' teachings to finding our direction. It is the first of several passages in this discourse where love for Jesus is defined by obedience to his word (vv. 21,23; 15:10).

14:16 *another Advocate.* The Greek term *paraclete* is a rich term for which there is no sufficient English translation. Attempts such as "advocate" or "helper" or "comforter" fall because they emphasize only one of many aspects of the term. The paraclete is a combination of witness to Jesus and counselor, teacher and helper for the disciples. The term refers to the Holy Spirit. ***forever.*** This is in contrast to the approximately three years of Jesus' earthly ministry.

14:17 *Spirit of truth.* This is another name for the Holy Spirit. ***whom the world cannot receive.*** When John refers to "the world" here, he means those who have the spirit of the world's values, in contrast to God's values. Those who had the spirit of the world rejected Christ, and therefore will reject the Holy Spirit sent to continue his work. ***abides with you ... will be in you.*** The reality of the indwelling Spirit lifts the Old Testament expectation of a new covenant, wherein God would dwell with his people and write his law "on their hearts" to unimaginable heights (Isa. 7:14; Jer. 31:31ff; Ezekiel 34:30).

14:18 *orphaned.* This promise is reminiscent of Galatians 4:6 where Paul says, "God has sent the Spirit of his Son into our hearts, crying, 'Abba! Father!' " The Spirit maintains this important family connection.

14:19 *you also will live.* This refers not only to the eternal aspect of the life they will have because of Christ's resurrection, but also to the quality of their life. After the Crucifixion, the disciples were dead spiritually. But they came back to life with the Resurrection.

14:20 *I am in my Father, and you in me ...*There is a mystical union of souls in Christ Jesus, a unity that contrasts the divergence and conflict of the world as it is without God.

What is the closest you have come to feeling "orphaned"?

Mother Teresa's Source of Direction. Mother Teresa received great accolades for her work with the poorest of the poor in Calcutta, India. But it was not such human affirmation that was her main source of comfort or motivation in what she did. It was the Spirit of God that was near to her and within her. Her biographer, Lush Gjergji, writes of her early work and how God directed her in it in the book, *Mother Teresa: Her Life, Her Works:*

"For a while she slept with the Little Sisters of the Poor. But sleep was short, because even during the night she went out among the homeless to visit and assist them. Like a night spirit the little woman in the sari sought out the abandoned, the dying and the lepers whom she could find everywhere, in the hovels and in the streets. Many had been cast out of the city by the healthy people, out of fear and repugnance. Besides taking care of the abandoned children she also had to contend with leprosy. She had to confront this calamity which people considered as a punishment from God.

"But let us go back to the children. Speaking of those times she said: 'Those were days of joy and happiness, but also of fatigue, of difficulties and serious trials.' This was for her a period of maturing faith, and of growth in her new mission, in a life of renunciation and weariness, in which she could count on God's help alone. This conviction developed as a result of her daily experience, in which God was her only strength and her one resource. It was from this situation that the following prayer emerged:

" 'O God, you are everything to me. Make use of me as you will. You caused me to leave the convent where I was at least a little useful; now guide me as you wish.'

"Surveying the unspeakable wretchedness that surrounded her alone, and without any resources, she addressed herself to God:

" 'O God, if I cannot help these people in their indigence and misfortune, at least let me die with them and near them, so that in this way I may bear witness to your love.' "[1]

---

[1] Lush Gjergji, *Mother Teresa: Her Life, Her Works* (Hyde Park, NY: New City Press, 1991), p. 45.

WEEK 7: EASTER 7

Opening Our Eyes to God's Protection

John 17:1–11

 **GATHERING**
10 min.

 **STUDY**
30 min.

 **CARING**
20–40 min.

Leader: The agenda has three parts. In the Gathering time you'll be getting to know each other through an "ice-breaker." This will be for your total group. The Study time has two parts: (1) Story and (2) Scripture. If you are short of time, skip the Story and move to the Scripture. Begin by reading out loud the Story or the Scripture to the whole group. Then divide into groups of 4 for the Study time. Finally, regather the total group for the Caring time. Keep to this agenda: (1) Gathering—10 minutes, (2) Study—30 minutes, and (3) Caring—20–40 minutes.

 **Scary Masks.** Psychologists tell us that one reason children like to wear scary masks is the principle of "identification with the aggressor"—if they are afraid of ghosts, they won't be quite as afraid of them if they can dress up as a ghost and be one themselves. Adults have different fears. But using the same principle, which of the following would you most like to dress up as?

DENTIST—with an evil grin and drill to stick in people's mouths

AUTO MECHANIC—with greasy overalls and a recording that says, "We found a little problem," over and over again

BIG CLOCK—that runs so fast, everyone is always late

COLLEGE STUDENT—with a recording that says, "Send money! Send money!"

FATHER TIME—complete with a big mirror that magnifies your wrinkles

POLICE OFFICER—with a light I can flash when I follow people

SMILING POLITICIAN—with a recording that says, "Trust me! Trust me!"

Opening Our Eyes to God's Protection
Easter 7 - John 17:1–11

PURPOSE

To see how, while we may face many dangers and even tragedies in this world, God does give us protection from that which would threaten our eternal well-being.

FOP THE PASTOR

The following material you can use as input for your sermon preparation on this week's Gospel Scripture from the book of John. For further input you may want to share and further comment on the story of Corrie ten Boom, which your study group(s) will be responding to during their session. Also, it's important to share in your sermon or homily your own response to the personal question (or other personally-oriented question) to model personal sharing for your congregation.

SCRIPTURE

17 *After Jesus had spoken these words, he looked up to heaven and said, "Father, the hour has come; glorify your Son so that the Son may glorify you, ²since you have given him authority over all people, to give eternal life to all whom you have given him. ³And this is eternal life, that they may know you, the only true God, and Jesus Christ whom you have sent. ⁴I glorified you on earth by finishing the work that you gave me to do. ⁵So now, Father, glorify me in your own presence with the glory that I had in your presence before the world existed.*

⁶"I have made your name known to those whom you gave me from the world. They were yours, and you gave them to me, and they have kept your word. ⁷Now they know that everything you have given me is from you; ⁸for the words that you gave to me I have given to them, and they have received them and know in truth that I came from you; and they have believed that you sent me. ⁹I am asking on their behalf; I am not asking on behalf of the world, but on behalf of those whom you gave me, because they are yours. ¹⁰All mine are yours, and yours are mine; and I have been glorified in them. ¹¹And now I am no longer in the world, but they are in the world, and I am coming to you. Holy Father, protect them in your name that you have given me, so that they may be one, as we are one.

John 17:1–11

INTRODUCTION

People look to all sorts of things to protect them today. Some keep guns. While that gives some a sense of security, it is also true that such guns are the source of many accidental shootings, making the source of protection also the source of danger. Some buy security systems. But those are often expensive, and make many people feel like prisoners in their own home. The police can help, but they are most often overworked and underfunded. Even so, none of these can truly keep danger from reaching us in a world where drive-by killers assault perfect strangers without warning. Can anything help? Only the oldest source of them all—putting ourselves into the hands of God! True, God does not keep dangers from coming into our life. But what God's protection does do is to assure us that "all things work together for good for those who love God, who are called according to his purpose" (Rom. 8:28). Even if tragedy strikes us, we understand God can use it for the good. Even if death overtakes us, we know that death is not the final victor in Christ Jesus (1 Cor. 15:54–57). That is the ultimate security system!

17:1 *your Son so that ...* The Son (Jesus) will be glorified, or given honor, when he completes what he came for—dying on the cross and then rising victorious over death. This will also glorify, or bring honor, to God because people will know that he has acted to save his people.

17:3 *this is eternal life.* Eternal life is inextricably bound with relationship—relationship to God, and to God's Son Jesus. While the synoptic Gospels refer mostly to "the kingdom of God," it is this eternal life that takes center stage in John.

17:4 *the work that you gave me to do.* Jesus has consistently defined his mission in terms of doing the works of the Father (5:17,19; 8:29; 10:31–32). By so doing, he has glorified God by revealing to people what the Father is like.

17:5 *the glory that I had in your presence ...* John consistently presents Jesus Christ as preexistent, and it is this glory he had before his earthly life and ministry that is referred to here (see 1:1–3; 8:58).

17:6 *those whom you gave me.* Just as God gave Jesus a task, he also gave him the disciples with whom to fulfill that task. In making good use of what he was given, Jesus serves as an example of stewardship.

17:8 *the words that you gave to me.* Again, all Jesus has was given by the Father, and he was the perfect steward.

17:9 *the world.* The "world" in John's Gospel has several meanings. While sometimes it means humanity in general ("For God so loved the world ...", 3:16), in chapters 13–17 it means those people and their systems that stand opposed to him and the Father (14:27; 15:18; 16:33.)

17:11 *protect them in your name.* Throughout the Old Testament, God's name was tied in with his power to deliver and save his people. Since this has been the purpose of Jesus' mission as well, that name has been given to him. This protection is not such that the disciples escape trouble, but that they maintain unity in the midst of the world. The unity for which Jesus prays in this section (vv. 11,21–23) is a unity reflecting that of the Father and Son (vv. 11,21) involving mutual love, commitment to the same mission, and loyalty to the truth of Christ.

When Jesus was going away to his Father, he gave the disciples the going-away gift of protection. Normally, however, when someone goes away, it is the other people who give them gifts. What is the best going-away gift you remember receiving?

Corrie ten Boom's Close Call. Corrie ten Boom and her family showed great faith in rescuing Jews from the Nazis during World War II. As a result they had to face the dangers of a Nazi concentration camp. Even before that they faced the dangers of war. But in the midst of all these dangers they found God to be a safe "Hiding Place." Corrie tells of one close call she had during the war, previous to being caught and sent to prison, in her book, *The Hiding Place:*

"One night I tossed for an hour while dogfights raged overhead, streaking my patch of sky with fire. At last I heard Betsie stirring in the kitchen and ran down to join her.

"She was making tea. She brought it into the dining room where we had covered the windows with heavy black paper and set out the best cups. Somewhere in the night there was an explosion; the dishes in the cupboard rattled. For an hour we sipped our tea and talked, until the sound of planes died away and the sky was silent. I said goodnight to Betsie at the door to Tante Jans' rooms and groped my way up the dark stairs to my own. The fiery light was gone from the sky. I felt for my bed: there was the pillow. Then in the darkness my hand closed over something hard. Sharp too! I felt blood trickle along a finger.

"It was a jagged piece of metal, ten inches long.

" 'Betsie!'

"I raced down the stairs with the shrapnel shard in my hand. We went back to the dining room and stared at it in the light while Betsie bandaged my hand. 'On your pillow,' she kept saying.

" 'Betsie, if I hadn't heard you in the kitchen—'

"But Betsie put a finger on my mouth. 'Don't say it, Corrie! There are no 'ifs' in God's world. And no places that are safer than other places. The center of His will is our only safety—O Corrie, let us pray that we may always know it!' "[1]

[1]Corrie ten Boom, *The Hiding Place* (Minneapolis, MN: World Wide Publications, 1971), pp. 84–85.

FALL SEASON
PENTECOST / ORDINARY TIME

Theme: "Responding to God's Call"

WEEK 1: PENTECOST 16
A Call to Reconciliation
Matthew 18:15–20

 **GATHERING** 10 min.    **STUDY** 30 min.    **CARING** 20–40 min.

Leader: The agenda has three parts. In the Gathering time you'll be getting to know each other through an "ice-breaker." This will be for your total group. The Study time has two parts: (1) Story and (2) Scripture. If you are short of time, skip the Story and move to the Scripture. Begin by reading out loud the Story or the Scripture to the whole group. Then divide into groups of 4 for the Study time. Finally, regather the total group for the Caring time. Keep to this agenda: (1) Gathering—10 minutes, (2) Study—30 minutes, and (3) Caring—20–40 minutes.

 **Childhood Wishes.** Have everyone in the group answer the first question. Then go around again on question #2.

1. Give your name and tell where you spent the largest part of your childhood.

2. When you were in the sixth grade, which of the following animals or things, all seen on television, would you have wished for?
   - ❏ the dolphin on *Flipper* as a playmate
   - ❏ Injun Joe's cave (*Tom Sawyer*) to explore
   - ❏ to be able to talk to animals like Dr. Doolittle
   - ❏ living in the tree house on *Swiss Family Robinson*
   - ❏ our own maid or butler, like on *The Brady Bunch* or *Family Affair*
   - ❏ Batman's "Batmobile"
   - ❏ the horse on *National Velvet*
   - ❏ Sky King's airplane

<table>
<tr><td>

SESSION

1

</td><td>

A Call to Reconciliation
Pentecost 16 - Matthew 18:15–20

</td></tr>
</table>

PURPOSE

To see how Christ calls us to find reconciliation with those around us.

FOR THE PASTOR

The following material you can use as input for your sermon preparation on this week's Gospel Scripture from the book of Matthew. For further input you may want to share and further comment on the story of Martin Luther King, Jr., which your study group(s) will be responding to during their session. Also, it's important to share in your sermon or homily your own response to the personal question (or other personally-oriented question) to model personal sharing for your congregation.

SCRIPTURE

[15]*"If another member of the church sins against you, go and point out the fault when the two of you are alone. If the member listens to you, you have regained that one.* [16]*But if you are not listened to, take one or two others along with you, so that every word may be confirmed by the evidence of two or three witnesses.* [17]*If the member refuses to listen to them, tell it to the church; and if the offender refuses to listen even to the church, let such a one be to you as a Gentile and a tax collector.* [18]*Truly I tell you, whatever you bind on earth will be bound in heaven, and whatever you loose on earth will be loosed in heaven.* [19]*Again, truly I tell you, if two of you agree on earth about anything you ask, it will be done for you by my Father in heaven.* [20]*For where two or three are gathered in my name, I am there among them."*

Matthew 18:15–20

INTRODUCTION

We live in a world of many divisions—division between men and women, division between young and old, divisions between different races and cultures. Division between the sexes seems to have accelerated of late, with "male-bashing" greeting cards, rap songs that denigrate women, and continued strife over women seeking entrance to traditionally male areas. Can reconciliation be found? Division between young and old has reached into the churches, with style of music in worship a main area of contention. Can reconciliation be found? The burning of African-American churches, and tension over immigration of Hispanics has continued a tragic tradition of division among racial and cultural lines in our country. And the Sunday morning worship hour remains the most segregated time in America. Can reconciliation be found? Only when we start talking to each other across these barriers, and listening with the ears of Christ, can reconciliation happen.

18:15 *when the two of you are alone.* Public confrontation requires both parties to "save face," and so little real reconciliation can be accomplished.

18:16 *one or two others.* Involving these others is based on the Old Testament Law's requirement that no case be settled without two or three witnesses (Deut. 19:15).

18:17 *tell it to the church.* Christians at this time took pride in not having to take such issues to secular courts. Of course, the other person also had the right to take the matter to the church, and the church might side with them. But in any case, the church was to be listened to. ***as a Gentile and a tax collector.*** These were the prime examples of outcast people in these times. This teaching became the basis for excommunication in the church. Paul also referred to excommunication under such circumstances (see 1 Cor. 5:3–5,9–13; 2 Cor. 13:1–3). But from the second century on Christians have been hesitant to employ this approach because of a fear of violating Jesus' teaching in 7:1–5 about judging people.

18:18–19 *whatever you bind on earth ...* This is a repeat of what Christ first said to Peter in 16:19. It is a declaration that church decisions regarding discipline of an erring member are made with divine authority and in the presence of Jesus. This is the ultimate reason why the admonition of the church is to be heeded.

18:20 *where two or three are gathered ...* This is not a general promise regarding prayer or worship as such, but a pronouncement that Jesus would be present when church decisions are made, lending his authority.

When you were a teenager, what was the most important thing you learned in your conflicts with your parents?

Martin Luther King, Jr. Converts a Foe. Martin Luther King, Jr. is known for his leadership role in helping to bring greater justice to African-Americans, and for his dream of reconciliation between the races. But the lessons he sought to teach the nation he first had to learn in his personal relationships. When King was in seminary, an incident in his personal life seemed like a type for what he would later confront on a national level. His biographer, Stephen Oates, tells about it in his book, *Let the Trumpet Sound: The Life of Martin Luther King, Jr.:*

"Back at the seminary, King had another brush with violence when a North Carolina white student came banging on his door one day. The student was well known for his racial views: he couldn't accept Negroes as his schoolmates and called them 'darkies.' Somebody had messed up his room—a prank called a 'room raid'—and he blamed King. He was in a tirade, shouting at King, hurling maledictions at him. Then he drew a pistol and threatened to shoot King dead. But King would not be rattled. Looking the maddened student in the eye, he calmly denied having anything to do with the room raid. By now the racket had attracted other students: they yelled at the North Carolinian, made him put his gun down. Afterward they brought the matter before the student government; but to everybody's surprise King refused to press charges. With students and faculty alike clamoring against him, though, the North Carolinian publicly admitted he was wrong and extended King an apology.

"After that King became the most popular student at Crozer, widely admired not only for his scholarship, but for his courage and grace as well. Certain of acceptance now, he began to relax some and get more involved in campus social life. What was more, he and the North Carolinian student eventually became friends. The entire episode seemed a valuable lesson in how to convert a foe into a comrade."[1]

[1] Stephen B. Oates, *Let the Trumpet Sound: The Life of Martin Luther King, Jr.* (New York: Harper Collins, 1982), pp. 29–30.

SERENDIPITY

Small Group
H A N D O U T

WEEK 2: PENTECOST 17
A Call to Forgiveness
Matthew 18:21–35

 **GATHERING**
10 min.

 **STUDY**
30 min.

 **CARING**
20–40 min.

Leader: The agenda has three parts. In the Gathering time you'll be getting to know each other through an "ice-breaker." This will be for your total group. The Study time has two parts: (1) Story and (2) Scripture. If you are short of time, skip the Story and move to the Scripture. Begin by reading out loud the Story or the Scripture to the whole group. Then divide into groups of 4 for the Study time. Finally, regather the total group for the Caring time. Keep to this agenda: (1) Gathering—10 minutes, (2) Study—30 minutes, and (3) Caring—20–40 minutes.

 **Life's Embarrassing Moments.** As you look back over your past, which of the following transitions brought you the most embarrassment? Tell as much as you can remember about your experience so we can blush right along with you!

- going to junior high and having to shower in front of other kids

- going to a junior high dance and getting up the nerve to ask someone to dance

- the first time I kissed someone of the opposite sex (outside the family)

- meeting my future in-laws for the first time and saying the wrong thing

- fixing that meal when we were first married and I tried a new recipe

- that time at my first job when I realized they don't teach you everything at school

- the day I realized my teenager didn't want me around in public

- meeting my teenage child's date and saying the wrong thing

A Call to Forgiveness
Pentecost 17 - Matthew 18:21–35

PURPOSE

To consider how Christ always calls us to forgive as we have been forgiven.

FOR THE PASTOR

The following material you can use as input for your sermon preparation on this week's Gospel Scripture from the book of Matthew. For further input you may want to share and further comment on the story of Corrie ten Boom, which your study group(s) will be responding to during their session. Also, it's important to share in your sermon or homily your own response to the personal question (or other personally-oriented question) to model personal sharing for your congregation.

SCRIPTURE

[21]Then Peter came and said to him, "Lord, if another member of the church sins against me, how often should I forgive? As many as seven times?" [22]Jesus said to him, "Not seven times, but, I tell you, seventy-seven times.

[23]"For this reason the kingdom of heaven may be compared to a king who wished to settle accounts with his slaves. [24]When he began the reckoning, one who owed him ten thousand talents was brought to him; [25]and, as he could not pay, his lord ordered him to be sold, together with his wife and children and all his possessions, and payment to be made. [26]So the slave fell on his knees before him, saying, 'Have patience with me, and I will pay you everything.' [27]And out of pity for him, the lord of that slave released him and forgave him the debt. [28]But that same slave, as he went out, came upon one of his fellow slaves who owed him a hundred denarii; and seizing him by the throat, he said, 'Pay what you owe.' [29]Then his fellow slave fell down and pleaded with him, 'Have patience with me, and I will pay you.' [30]But he refused; then he went and threw him into prison until he would pay the debt. [31]When his fellow slaves saw what had happened, they were greatly distressed, and they went and reported to their lord all that had taken place. [32]Then his lord summoned him and said to him, 'You wicked slave! I forgave you all that debt because you pleaded with me. [33]Should you not have had mercy on your fellow slave, as I had mercy on you?' [34]And in anger his lord handed him over to be tortured until he would pay his entire debt. [35]So my heavenly Father will also do to every one of you, if you do not forgive your brother or sister from your heart."

Matthew 18:21–35

INTRODUCTION

We find so many ways to inflict pain on each other—divorce, child abuse, spousal abuse, adultery and the deceitful and destructive behavior that goes with addiction, to name a few. What the Bible is bold to proclaim, however, is that none of us have more to forgive than God has already forgiven us. This is true because every affront against God's children is also an affront against him. Therefore the offenses pile up exponentially. Yet, the Good News of Jesus Christ is that God forgives us all of that! And even better, he gives us his power and love to forgive others, if we are but willing. This may not make forgiveness easy, especially if the hurts created are deep. And in many instances, like with abuse or repeated infidelity, a person is wise to question whether the other person should be trusted again. Nevertheless, a real forgiveness, where hate and bitterness is no longer held in the heart and where we can wish the other person good things, is possible, and it is possible because the forgiving love of God is available to us.

18:21 *how often should I forgive?* The rabbis taught that a person ought to be forgiven for a particular offense up to three times. After that, the offended person was under no obligation to grant forgiveness. Realizing that Jesus had a greater sense of mercy than was typical for rabbis, Peter doubled the traditional amount and added one more time for good measure! Since seven was the number of perfection, Peter may have thought that anyone who forgave someone that many times would be a spiritually perfect person.

18:22 *seventy-seven times.* This could also be understood as seven times seventy. Whichever reading is correct, Jesus explodes any notion of a limit to forgiveness! It is probable that "seventy-seven" is correct since it is the same number found in the Greek version of the OT story of Lamech.

18:23 *settle accounts.* Kings entrusted their day-to-day affairs to the management of servants. Such a servant might have been responsible for collecting the tax revenue for the king. This was an audit to check on how the servants were doing with respect to their management.

18:24 *ten thousand talents.* This is an impossibly high amount, comparable to a middle class American today being billions of dollars in debt.

18:25 *ordered him to be sold ...* Oriental kings had total power. Thus he decided to sell the man and his family into slavery to recover at least part of his losses.

18:27 *out of pity.* This same word, translated as "compassion," is used to describe the attitude of Jesus toward those in need (9:36; 15:32; 20:34). ***forgave him the debt.*** He stepped beyond what the slave had asked—to have patience with his repayment of a debt that would have been impossible for him to repay, and forgave the entire huge debt! This would have been a shocking statement, but would have been an obvious allusion to the enormity of the "debt" that God has forgiven us.

18:28 *a hundred denarii.* Since a denarii was a day's wage for a laborer, this was a reasonably large amount. However, it was nothing compared to what the first servant had been forgiven by the king.

18:29 Like the first servant, the second servant promises to repay the debt. Whereas this was an impossible promise for the first servant, in this case repayment could have been made over time.

18:30 *threw him into prison.* In a debtor's prison, the man's assets would be sold in order to make payment.

18:34 *to be tortured.* Prisoners were tortured to make them reveal hidden sources of money. ***until he would pay.*** Given the amount owed, the man would be in prison until death.

PERSONAL QUESTION

Who in your life, besides God, has seemingly forgiven you seventy-seven times?

STORY

Corrie ten Boom Forgives an S.S. Guard. Corrie ten Boom and her family sheltered Jews from the Nazis during World War II, and for that act of conscience she and others were sent to the Nazi concentration camps. In those camps her father and her sister Betsie died, and she suffered tremendous pain and degradation. But it was the presence of God that pulled her through. After she was released and the war ended, she went out speaking to groups about the love and presence of God in difficult times. But one of the hardest things she had to face happened on one of those early speaking tours—she was called on to forgive one of her former jailers. She tells the story of what happened in her autobiographical book, *The Hiding Place:*

"It was at a church service in Munich that I saw him, the former S.S. man who had stood guard at the shower room door in the processing center at Ravensbruck. He was the first of our actual jailers that I had seen since that time. And suddenly it was all there—the roomful of mocking men, the heaps of clothing, Betsie's pain-blanched face.

"He came up to me as the church was emptying, beaming and bowing. 'How grateful I am for your message, Fraulein,' he said. 'To think that, as you say, He has washed my sins away!'

"His hand was thrust out to shake mine. And I, who had preached so often to the people in Bloemendaal the need to forgive, kept my hand at my side.

"Even as the angry, vengeful thoughts boiled through me, I saw the sin of them. Jesus Christ had died for this man; was I going to ask for more? Lord Jesus, I prayed, forgive me and help me to forgive him.

"I tried to smile, I struggled to raise my hand. I could not. I felt nothing, not the slightest spark of warmth or charity. And so again I breathed a silent prayer. Jesus, I cannot forgive him. Give me Your forgiveness.

"As I took his hand the most incredible thing happened. From my shoulder along my arm and through my hand a current seemed to pass from me to him, while into my heart sprang a love for this stranger that almost overwhelmed me."[1]

---

[1] Corrie ten Boom, *The Hiding Place* (Minneapolis, MN: World Wide Publications, 1971), pp. 232–233.

Small Group
HANDOUT

WEEK 3: PENTECOST 18
A Call to Grace
Matthew 20:1–16

 **GATHERING**
10 min.

 **STUDY**
30 min.

 **CARING**
20–40 min.

Leader: The agenda has three parts. In the Gathering time you'll be getting to know each other through an "ice-breaker." This will be for your total group. The Study time has two parts: (1) Story and (2) Scripture. If you are short of time, skip the Story and move to the Scripture. Begin by reading out loud the Story or the Scripture to the whole group. Then divide into groups of 4 for the Study time. Finally, regather the total group for the Caring time. Keep to this agenda: (1) Gathering—10 minutes, (2) Study—30 minutes, and (3) Caring—20–40 minutes.

 **The Ideal Church.** Congratulations! You have just been selected as a committee of one to design the ideal church! In order to move plans along, the Board needs to know your decisions in the following areas (each person answer #1, then move on to #2):

1. What would you like to call this church? (Choose a name and a motto.)
   - ❏ The Come-as-You-Are Church—"It's not what you wear; it's who you are!"
   - ❏ The Old-Time Gospel Church—"Return to traditional values!"
   - ❏ The Nike Church—"Stop talking, and just do it!"
   - ❏ The House of Love—(Borrowing from Amy Grant)—"We'll keep the light on!"

2. Apart from belief in Christ, what would be the philosophical basis of this church?
   - ❏ Four hugs a day are necessary for health!
   - ❏ Worship is not a spectator sport!
   - ❏ Spiritual strugglers are welcome!
   - ❏ Check your ego at the door!

<table>
<tr><td>SESSION
3</td><td><h1>A Call to Grace</h1>Pentecost 18 - Matthew 20:1–16</td></tr>
</table>

PURPOSE

To see how responding to God's call means responding to a call of grace that helps us deal with our weakness.

FOR THE PASTOR

The following material you can use as input for your sermon preparation on this week's Gospel Scripture from the book of Matthew. For further input you may want to share and further comment on the story of Thomas Merton, which your study group(s) will be responding to during their session. Also, it's important to share in your sermon or homily your own response to the personal question (or other personally-oriented question) to model personal sharing for your congregation.

SCRIPTURE

20 *"For the kingdom of heaven is like a landowner who went out early in the morning to hire laborers for his vineyard. [2]After agreeing with the laborers for the usual daily wage, he sent them into his vineyard. [3]When he went out about nine o'clock, he saw others standing idle in the marketplace; [4]and he said to them, 'You also go into the vineyard, and I will pay you whatever is right.' So they went. [5]When he went out again about noon and about three o'clock, he did the same. [6]And about five o'clock he went out and found others standing around; and he said to them, 'Why are you standing here idle all day?' [7]They said to him 'Because no one has hired us.' He said to them, 'You also go into the vineyard.' [8]When evening came, the owner of the vineyard said to his manager, 'Call the laborers and give them their pay, beginning with the last and then going to the first.' [9]When those hired about five o'clock came, each of them received the usual daily wage. [10]Now when the first came, they thought they would receive more; but each of them also received the usual daily wage. [11]And when they received it, they grumbled against the landowner, [12]saying, 'These last worked only one hour, and you have made them equal to us who have borne the burden of the day and the scorching heat. [13]But he replied to one of them, 'Friend, I am doing you no wrong; did you not agree with me for the usual daily wage? [14]Take what belongs to you and go; I choose to give to this last the same as I give to you. [15]Am I not allowed to do what I choose with what belongs to me? Or are you envious because I am generous?' [16]So the last will be first, and the first will be last."*

Matthew 20:1–16

INTRODUCTION

When you are wanting to be part of a group, one of the first things you need to know is how that group operates; and at the heart of how the church is to operate is the principle of grace. Ours is not to be an everyone-for-themselves-and-try-to-out-perform-the-others operation. We are to perform as one. As such we must remember that everyone has been invited to be part of the team, not because of their GPA in school, or because of their "minor league stats," or because of any performance measure, but because God has chosen us. God chooses us to be part of his team because he loves us, and God knows we find our greatest meaning working for him. Similarly, our reward is not to "move up the hierarchy" or to move up a notch on the pay scale. The reward is the same for all—to be part of the eternal fellowship of the family of God. We cannot say we deserve more than the others on the team, because the reality is that none of us deserves to be on the team in the first place. We have our status on the basis of grace—the unmerited favor of God. Responding to God's call as part of the church, then starts with that understanding. Only if we are willing to be on a team of equals—people equally under grace—need we apply for this position.

20:1 *to hire laborers.* Landowners had full-time servants who took care of the daily needs of the estate, but at certain times (such as planting, pruning or harvest) he would hire day laborers to help with work that the regular servants could not do on their own. At these times, men would gather in the village and hope that they might be hired for the day.

20:2 *After agreeing with the laborers.* The implication was that this was a negotiated arrangement. Bargaining back and forth was a common way for people in the Middle East to do business as offers and counter-offers would be made. Since the landowner needs workers for that day, the laborers are in a position to negotiate a bit. Eventually they agreed on a denarius, which was the usual daily wage.

20:3 *the marketplace.* This was the gathering place for a village. People would meet there not only to buy and sell, but to socialize as well. It would be a natural place for people looking for work to go in hopes of meeting someone who would be able to hire them.

20:4 *whatever is right.* Since these workers had no reasonable prospects for work that day, they were not in much of a position to bargain. Whatever the landowners paid them would be better than nothing. There is no negotiation about the wage; only the promise that it will be just.

20:5 *three o'clock.* By this time, these workers would have no expectation of getting work that day.

20:6 *five o'clock.* The listeners would have been surprised to hear of the landowner still hiring people to work this late in the day.

20:8 *when evening came.* This would be at dusk. The laborer's day went from sunrise to sunset. According to the Old Testament law, workers were to be paid their wages at the end of the day so that they would not have to go hungry (Deut. 24:14–15).

PERSONAL QUESTION

Who is the most generous employer you have ever worked for?

STORY

Thomas Merton Responds to God's Call. Thomas Merton was raised as a Protestant, but in a family where God was relegated to the sidelines of life. When he entered adulthood he had little or no religious faith. But over time he began to understand this as a void in his life. He was eventually led to the Catholic Church, where he became a Trappist monk. He experienced God's grace most intimately in his First Communion. He describes his experience in his book, *The Seven Storey Mountain:*

"The priest, and Christ in him ... breathed again into my face.

" 'Thomas, receive the good Spirit through this breathing, and receive the Blessing of God. Peace be with thee.'

"Then he began again to pray, and sign me with Crosses ... and finally he poured the water on my head, and named me Thomas, 'if thou be not already baptized.'

"After that, I went into the confessional, where one of the other assistants was waiting for me. I knelt in the shadows. ... 'Poor man,' I thought. He seemed very young and he had always looked so innocent to me that I wondered how he was going to identify and understand the things I was about to tell him.

"But one by one ... I tore out all those sins by their roots, like teeth. ...

"I did not have any time to feel how relieved I was when I came stumbling out. ... But ever since that day, I have loved confessionals.

"... when the little bells were rung I knew what was happening. And I saw the raised Host—the silence and simplicity with which Christ once again triumphed, raised up, drawing all things to Himself—drawing me to Himself. ...

"... Father Moore turned around and made a big cross in absolution, and held up the little Host.

" 'Behold the Lamb of God: behold Him Who taketh away the sins of the world.'

"And my First Communion began to come towards me, down the steps. I was the only one at the altar rail. Heaven was entirely mine—that Heaven in which sharing makes no division or diminution."[1]

[1]Thomas Merton, *The Seven Storey Mountain* , pp. 248–249. © Harcourt, Brace & Company. All rights reserved.

Small Group
HANDOUT

WEEK 4: PENTECOST 19

A Call to Action

Matthew 21:23–32

 **GATHERING** 10 min.　　 **STUDY** 30 min.　　 **CARING** 20–40 min.

Leader: The agenda has three parts. In the Gathering time you'll be getting to know each other through an "ice-breaker." This will be for your total group. The Study time has two parts: (1) Story and (2) Scripture. If you are short of time, skip the Story and move to the Scripture. Begin by reading out loud the Story or the Scripture to the whole group. Then divide into groups of 4 for the Study time. Finally, regather the total group for the Caring time. Keep to this agenda: (1) Gathering—10 minutes, (2) Study—30 minutes, and (3) Caring—20–40 minutes.

 **Adult (not X-rated!) Video Games.** The following are new video games that have been developed for the adult mind and experience. Which would you be most interested in? Share your response with your group!

PAC-MAN 2 (the sequel)—he eats an energy dot, then gobbles up obnoxious politicians

WHERE IN THE WORLD IS (your name)?—this game gets you lost in some far corner of the world so your boss or demanding family members can't find you

VIRTUAL REALITY HOUSE CLEANING—if the house is a mess, put on the special goggles and you won't know the difference

SIMTEENAGER—build your own teen, exactly like you want, and if he or she still gives you lip, just select "edit"

SIMBODY—build the body you want without diets or exercises

TELE-TERMINATOR—seeks out the location of telephone solicitors and sends out a big macho guy to make them a deal they can't refuse

<table>
<tr><td>

SESSION

4
</td><td>

A Call to Action
Pentecost 19 - Matthew 21:23–32
</td></tr>
</table>

PURPOSE

To consider how responding to God's call means not just acknowledging a belief or truth, but responding in action.

FOR THE PASTOR

The following material you can use as input for your sermon preparation on this week's Gospel Scripture from the book of Matthew. For further input you may want to share and further comment on the story of Albert Schweitzer, which your study group(s) will be responding to during their session. Also, it's important to share in your sermon or homily your own response to the personal question (or other personally-oriented question) to model personal sharing for your congregation.

SCRIPTURE

[23]*"When he entered the temple, the chief priests and the elders of the people came to him as he was teaching, and said "By what authority are you doing these things, and who gave you this authority?"* [24]*Jesus said to them, "I will also ask you one question; if you tell me the answer, then I will also tell you by what authority I do these things.* [25]*Did the baptism of John come from heaven, or was it of human origin?" And they argued with one another, "If we say, 'From heaven,' he will say to us, 'Why then did you not believe him?'* [26]*But if we say, 'Of human origin,' we are afraid of the crowd; for all regard John as a prophet."* [27]*So they answered Jesus, "We do not know." And he said to them, "Neither will I tell you by what authority I am doing these things.*

[28]*"What do you think? A man had two sons; he went to the first and said, 'Son, go and work in the vineyard today.'* [29]*He answered, 'I will not'; but later he changed his mind and went.* [30]*The father went to the second and said the same; and he answered 'I go, sir'; but he did not go.* [31]*Which of the two did the will of his father?" They said, "The first." Jesus said to them. "Truly I tell you, the tax collectors and the prostitutes are going into the kingdom of God ahead of you.* [32]*For John came to you in the way of righteousness and you did not believe him, but the tax collectors and the prostitutes believed him; and even after you saw it, you did not change your minds and believe him."*

Matthew 21:23–32

The church can never be what it was meant to be if all we do is study, discuss and listen. It's not that such activities aren't important. They are. We need to continually learn more about who Jesus is, what the church is called to be, and how we fit in as individuals. But if all we do is study the issues, the world will continue on a downhill slide, and God's vision for a redeemed creation will suffer. God calls us to action as his church. He calls us to get out of our church buildings into the world to feed the hungry, clothe the naked, visit the imprisoned and bring good news to the downhearted. Theologian Harvey Cox has said that when we don't take action, it even makes our Christian study times more boring. He writes, "A parachutist gets interested in training when he has to jump the next day. He better learns how the parachute operates if tomorrow he is going to bail out at 20,000 feet. For him the training session ... is not boring at all. ... On the other hand, we are bored by our training sessions because we never jump. We don't jump into the place we are needed for reconciliation, where we are needed to be poured out."[1] Responding to God's call then must mean responding to a call to action.

21:23 *the chief priests and the elders.* The chief priests were the key officers of the temple, just below the High Priest in rank. The elders were powerful and (reputedly) wise leaders of Israel. They were generally not priests but instead were administrators, judges, military leaders, etc.

21:24 *I will also ask you.* Answering a question with a question was a common tactic in rabbinic debate.

21:25–27 They know that no matter how they answer, Jesus has turned the tables upon them. To acknowledge that John's authority came from God ("from heaven") would be to admit that John was a true prophet. If this were so, then they would have to accept that Jesus came from God, since that was John's testimony. On the other hand, to deny that John was a prophet would incur the anger of the crowds, who had believed in him.

21:31 *Which of the two ...?* This parable, unique to Matthew, shows that it is not words that matter, but actions. ***the tax collectors and the prostitutes.*** In this society, these two groups of people represented the lowest depths to which men and women respectively could sink. For Jesus to say such people entered the kingdom of God at all would have sounded scandalous, but for him to say such people were entering the kingdom ahead of the religious authorities was outlandish!

Who has played the role of "chief priests and elders" in your life, the one or ones who gave you a hard time or sought to bring you down?

Albert Schweitzer Switches from Talk to Action. Albert Schweitzer, in the early part of his life was building a reputation as a renowned scholar and musician. He also was an ordained minister. But these activities did not satisfy his desire to be part of God's work with people in need. So at age 30 he went back to school to become a medical doctor with the specific plan to go to Africa as a medial missionary. The story of his work in that capacity has become legendary. In his autobiographical book, *Out of My Life and Thought,* he tells of his motivations:

"I wanted to be a doctor so that I might be able to work without having to talk. For years I had been giving of myself in words, and it was with joy that I had followed the calling of theological teacher and preacher. But this new form of activity would consist not in preaching the religion of love, but in practicing it. Medical knowledge would make it possible for me to carry out my intention in the best and most complete way, wherever the path of service might lead me.

"Given my choice of equatorial Africa, acquiring this knowledge was especially appropriate because in the district to which I planned to go a doctor was, according to the missionaries' reports, the most urgent of all its needs. In their reports and magazines they always regretted that they could not provide help for the Africans who came in great physical pain. I was greatly motivated to study medicine and become, one day, the doctor whom these unhappy people needed. Whenever I was tempted to feel that the years I should have to sacrifice were too long, I reminded myself that Hamilcar and Hannibal had prepared for their march on Rome by their slow and tedious conquest of Spain."[2]

[1]Harvey Cox, *God's Revolution and Man's Responsibility* (Valley Forge, PA: The Judson Press, 1965), p.118.
[2]Albert Schweitzer, *Out of My Life and Thought* (New York: Henry Holt & Co., 1949), p. 92.

WEEK 5: PENTECOST 20
A Call to Stewardship
Matthew 21:33–46

 **GATHERING** 10 min.    **STUDY** 30 min.    **CARING** 20–40 min.

Leader: The agenda has three parts. In the Gathering time you'll be getting to know each other through an "ice-breaker." This will be for your total group. The Study time has two parts: (1) Story and (2) Scripture. If you are short of time, skip the Story and move to the Scripture. Begin by reading out loud the Story or the Scripture to the whole group. Then divide into groups of 4 for the Study time. Finally, regather the total group for the Caring time. Keep to this agenda: (1) Gathering—10 minutes, (2) Study—30 minutes, and (3) Caring—20–40 minutes.

Child Prodigies. For each of the categories below pick someone from your group who you think might have been a "child prodigy" by excelling in that area. Everyone in the group should be assigned by the others to one of the categories. Then each person should share how appropriate the group's judgment was to their childhood experience:

____________ smuggling stray animals into the house

____________ having and surviving childhood accidents

____________ making up imaginative excuses for misbehavior

____________ talking at an early age

____________ climbing the highest trees in the neighborhood

____________ watching horror movies without having nightmares

____________ inventing imaginative games that the other children wanted to play

____________ going through the most new clothes in a year

<table>
<tr><td>SESSION
5</td><td><h1>A Call to Stewardship</h1>Pentecost 20 - Matthew 21:33–46</td></tr>
</table>

PURPOSE

To appreciate how responding to God's call means being good stewards of all that has been entrusted to us.

FOR THE PASTOR

The following material you can use as input for your sermon preparation on this week's Gospel Scripture from the book of Matthew. For further input you may want to share and further comment on the story of Oscar Romero, which your study group(s) will be responding to during their session. Also, it's important to share in your sermon or homily your own response to the personal question (or other personally-oriented question) to model personal sharing for your congregation.

SCRIPTURE

[33]*"Listen to another parable. There was a landowner who planted a vineyard, put a fence around it, dug a wine press in it, and built a watchtower. Then he leased it to tenants and went to another country.* [34]*When the harvest time had come, he sent his slaves to the tenants to collect his produce.* [35]*But the tenants seized his slaves and beat one, killed another, and stoned another.* [36]*Again he sent other slaves, more than the first; and they treated them in the same way.* [37]*Finally he sent his son to them, saying, 'They will respect my son.'* [38]*But when the tenants saw the son, they said to themselves, 'This is the heir; come, let us kill him and get his inheritance.'* [39]*So they seized him, threw him out of the vineyard, and killed him.* [40]*Now when the owner of the vineyard comes, what will he do to those tenants?"* [41]*They said to him, "He will put those wretches to a miserable death, and lease the vineyard to other tenants who will give him the produce at harvest time."*

[42]*Jesus said to them, "Have you never read in the scriptures:*
> *'The stone that the builders rejected*
> *has become the cornerstone;*
> *this was the Lord's doing,*
> *and it is amazing in our eyes'?*

[43]*Therefore I tell you, the kingdom of God will be taken away from you and given to a people that produces the fruits of the kingdom.* [44]*The one who falls on this stone will be broken to pieces; and it will crush anyone on whom it falls."*

[45]*When the chief priests and the Pharisees heard his parables, they realized that he was speaking about them.* [46]*They wanted to arrest him, but they feared the crowds, because they regarded him as a prophet.*

Matthew 21:33–46

Some classic comedy routines have centered around people who have borrowed from friends, and then forgot who borrowed what. Dagwood and his neighbor Herb used to borrow so much from each other that they each needed a wheelbarrow to go get their things whenever they had a fight! In an old "Dick Van Dyke" segment Rob Petrie stews the whole show over how to remind Buddy that Buddy has borrowed money from him, only to find in the end that he really owed money to Buddy! In this same way, we often forget that what we have is borrowed—borrowed from our God who created it all. We own nothing. Because it is all borrowed from our God, we are responsible to God for how we use what has been entrusted to us, whether we are talking about physical property, personal abilities, or a given moment in time. That truth is what is meant by stewardship. We are called, individually and corporately, to respond to God's call to be stewards. In this session, we will look at what that means for us personally.

NOTES ON THE TEXT

21:33 *vineyard.* Grapes were one of the major crops in Israel. They were eaten fresh, made into raisins, boiled into a syrup, or made into wine. This particular vineyard was carefully built with a fence around it to keep out animals, a press in which to crush the grapes to make wine, and a tower where the farmer kept a lookout for robbers, and slept during the harvest. ***went to another country.*** Absentee landlords were common in the first century, especially in Galilee. Such a landlord would get tenant-farmers to work his large estate, requiring them to give him a portion of their harvest in payment for use of the land.

21:34 *slaves.* In terms of this parable, the servants represent the OT prophets, many of whom were killed. Tradition holds that Isaiah was executed by being sawn in two. Jeremiah faced many struggles, including being cast into a cistern to starve, and being taken as a prisoner to Egypt where tradition teaches he was killed.

21:37 *he sent his son.* Matthew's readers would have known this to be Jesus.

21:38 *get his inheritance.* The arrival of the son was mistakenly understood by the slaves as a sign that the landowner had died. Assuming that the son had come to claim his inheritance, they decided to take action. By law, a piece of ownerless property could be kept by those who first occupied and cultivated it. Since the tenants assumed the land would be ownerless if the son were dead, they plotted to kill him in order to lay claim to the land for themselves.

21:42 *The stone that the builders rejected ...* The reference is to a stone that was rejected in the building of the sanctuary of Solomon's temple which was later found to be the keystone to the porch (a keystone held an arch in place). This quote (Psalm 118:22) refers to how God established David as king even when his enemies attempted to defeat him. Later, rabbis had interpreted the stone to refer to Abraham, David or the Messiah. Here the stone is the Messiah (Jesus) whom the builders (the leaders) fail to recognize.

21:44 This verse carries allusions to both Isaiah 8:14–15 and Daniel 2:44–45. In both passages, either God or God's kingdom is pictured as a rock that trips up or crushes those who oppose God.

<table>
<tr><td>PERSONAL QUESTION</td><td>When you were in junior high, how likely were your parents or guardians to entrust important things (like care of the house while they were at work) to you?</td></tr>
<tr><td>STORY</td><td>Oscar Romero Calls "Tenants" to Account. In this imperfect world much is often entrusted into the hands of those who prove to be poor stewards; and Jesus' story, which we will later look at, of "tenants" who are willing to kill to retain control of that over which they are supposed to be stewards, is far from rare. In El Salvador, Archbishop Oscar Romero was one who sought to call the tenants to account. Eventually he himself was killed, like the messengers in the parable. Previous to that time, however, he fought against the violence. James Brockman tells the story in The Word Remains: The Life of Oscar Romero.</td></tr>
</table>

"On December 1, Romero said mass for a group of mothers of disappeared persons. The families of those who have disappeared, who may be dead but could be alive, who may be locked in dungeons or suffering beatings and indignities, are perhaps those who suffer most. They have not even the relief of mourning, living as they do between hope and hopelessness.

"Romero proposed the models of the mother in the book of Maccabees, who encouraged her seven sons to die rather than betray their faith in the living God, and of Mary, who stood under the cross of her son. 'Like Mary at the foot of the cross, every mother who suffers the outrage done to her child is a denunciation. Mary, the sorrowing mother, before the power of Pontius Pilate who has unjustly killed her son, is the cry of justice, of love, of peace, of what God wills, in the face of what God does not will, in the face of outrage, in the face of what should not be.'

"Preaching thus, he said, is not politics, but, rather, denouncing sin. 'This is the voice of justice, this is the voice of love, this is the cry that the church takes up from so many wives, mothers, homes, forsaken ones, in order to say: this should not be, return these sons and daughters as the law of God, the law of the Lord, demands. This is the cry against sin. This is what the church is doing, crying out against the sin that enthrones itself in history, in the life of the nation.' "[1]

[1] James Brockman, *The Word Remans: The Life of Oscar Romero* (Mary Knoll, NY: Orbis, 1982), p. 215.

Small Group
HANDOUT

WEEK 6: PENTECOST 21
A Call to Standards
Matthew 22:1–14

 **GATHERING**
10 min.

 **STUDY**
30 min.

 **CARING**
20–40 min.

Leader: The agenda has three parts. In the Gathering time you'll be getting to know each other through an "ice-breaker." This will be for your total group. The Study time has two parts: (1) Story and (2) Scripture. If you are short of time, skip the Story and move to the Scripture. Begin by reading out loud the Story or the Scripture to the whole group. Then divide into groups of 4 for the Study time. Finally, regather the total group for the Caring time. Keep to this agenda: (1) Gathering—10 minutes, (2) Study—30 minutes, and (3) Caring—20–40 minutes.

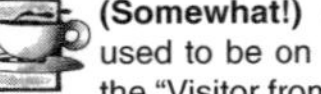 **(Somewhat!) Auspicious Titles.** When Johnny Carson used to be on *The Tonight Show* one of his characters was the "Visitor from the East" who Ed Mc Mahon would introduce using a series of titles, like "former financial advisor to Ivan Boesky." Which of the following titles would you find to be appropriate for the other members of your group? Write the name of one group member next to each title, and then focusing on one group member at a time, share what titles the others chose.

___________ former backup drummer to "the Energizer Bunny"

___________ chef to the Japanese sumo-wrestling team

___________ personal psychoanalyst for Daffy Duck

___________ former shop teacher for Tim "the Tool Man" Taylor

___________ former speech writer for Harpo Marx

___________ chief animal control officer at Jurassic Park

___________ jewelry buyer for Deion Sanders

___________ former charm school teacher for Roseanne

___________ former weight trainer for Don Knotts

<table>
<tr><td>SESSION
</td><td><h1>A Call to Standards</h1>Pentecost 21 - Matthew 22:1–14</td></tr>
</table>

PURPOSE

To consider how responding to God's call involves reaching for a higher standard than the world's standards.

FOR THE PASTOR

The following material you can use as input for your sermon preparation on this week's Gospel Scripture from the book of Matthew. For further input you may want to share and further comment on the story of Thomas Merton, which your study group(s) will be responding to during their session. Also, it's important to share in your sermon or homily your own response to the personal question (or other personally-oriented question) to model personal sharing for your congregation.

SCRIPTURE

22 *Once more Jesus spoke to them in parables, saying: [2]"The kingdom of heaven may be compared to a king who gave a wedding banquet for his son. [3]He sent his slaves to call those who had been invited to the wedding banquet, but they would not come. [4]Again he sent other slaves, saying, 'Tell those who have been invited: Look, I have prepared my dinner, my oxen and my fat calves have been slaughtered, and everything is ready; come to the wedding banquet.' [5]But they made light of it and went away, one to his farm, another to his business, [6]while the rest seized his slaves, mistreated them, and killed them. [7]The king was enraged. He sent his troops, destroyed those murderers, and burned their city. [8]Then he said to his slaves, 'The wedding is ready, but those invited were not worthy. [9]Go therefore into the main streets, and invite everyone you find to the wedding banquet.' [10]Those slaves went out into the streets and gathered all whom they found, both good and bad; so the wedding hall was filled with guests.*

[11]"But when the king came in to see the guests, he noticed a man there who was not wearing a wedding robe, [12]and he said to him, 'Friend, how did you get in here without a wedding robe?' And he was speechless. [13]Then the king said to the attendants, 'Bind him hand and foot, and throw him into the outer darkness, where there will be weeping and gnashing of teeth.' [14]For many are called, but few are chosen."

Matthew 22:1–14

INTRODUCTION

In an earlier session we talked about how God's call is a call to grace, and it is. But some people talk as if that means God has lowered his standards. Whatever we do is okay because we are "only human" and are saved by grace. It's like the story about a man who drove in one part of the country where he saw bull's eyes on all of the barns, and in the center of each bull's eye was an arrow. He said to himself, "What amazing archers these people must be!" He went up to one of the farmers to find their secret. He said, "Where did the people around here learn to shoot so well? Everywhere I look I see bull's eyes with arrows right in the middle!" The farmer said, "Oh, it ain't so amazing. We just shoot our arrow at the barn, and wherever it hits we draw a bull's eye around it!" Well, the moral standards of God's people cannot be that way. We cannot change the standard to fit our performance. We are certainly saved by grace, but God calls those who are saved to a high standard of morality—to love God, self and others in the way Christ loved. Responding to God's call means reaching for that standard.

22:3 *sent his slaves.* In well-to-do circles, invitations for banquets were issued well in advance, but the specific time to arrive was communicated on the day of the event when everything was ready. ***but they would not come.*** To reject a king's invitation was tantamount to rebellion. This attitude reflects that of the religious leaders who refused to truly practice God's law.

22:4–6 The insult is increased. When the king sends other slaves to repeat the invitation, they are snubbed or beaten! The slaves are meant to represent the Old Testament prophets.

22:9 *everyone you find.* The people who would be "hanging around" the streets would have been the social outcasts reduced to begging for survival. The irony is highlighted because it was just such people who were thought of as unworthy of such a feast.

22:11–12 *a wedding robe*. Guests would wear a freshly washed garment to a wedding. On some occasions, the host would provide garments appropriate for being worn in the presence of the king. In this allegorical parable, the wedding clothes represent the robes of righteousness God provides for his people (Zech. 3:3–5; Rev. 3:4,5,18).

22:13 *weeping and gnashing of teeth.* This is a stock phrase used to indicate the judgment of God. One should not take this parable too literally at this point, as if God is ready to throw people into hell for wearing the wrong garment! Certainly anyone who would do such a thing because of a social faux pas at a wedding would be thought of as a vicious tyrant. However, when we remember that what is being symbolized is a person who refused to "clothe himself or herself" in the righteousness of God's love, then God's wrath becomes more understandable.of leprosy for the equally dangerous disease of ingratitude.

When do you remember throwing a banquet or party that really "bombed"? What happened and how did you react?

STORY

Thomas Merton Sets His Sights High. Thomas Merton grew up in a family that was nominally Protestant, and really had little religious faith. When he became an adult, however, he began to be torn by religious questions, and eventually was attracted to Catholicism and became not only a priest, but a Trappist monk. The story of his spiritual pilgrimage, *The Seven Storey Mountain*, is one of the great spiritual autobiographies of our time. In it he tells how after converting to Catholicism he considered his own personal spiritual goals. He writes:

"... I forget what we were arguing about, but in the end Lax suddenly turned around and asked me the question:

" 'What do you want to be anyway?'...

" 'I don't know; I guess what I want is to be a good Catholic.'

" 'What do you mean, you want to be a good Catholic?'

"The explanation I gave was lame enough, and expressed my confusion, and betrayed how little I had really thought about it at all.

"Lax did not accept it.

" 'What you should say'—he told me—'what you should say is that you want to be a saint.'

"A saint! The thought struck me as a little weird. I said:

" 'How do you expect me to become a saint?'

" 'By wanting to,' said Lax simply.

" 'I can't be a saint,' I said, 'I can't be a saint.' And my mind darkened with a confusion of realities and unrealities: the knowledge of my own sins, and the false humility which makes men say that they cannot do the things that they must do, cannot reach the level that they must reach: the cowardice that says, 'I am satisfied to save my soul, to keep out of mortal sin,' but which means, by those words: 'I do not want to give up my sins and my attachments.'[1]

---

[1] Thomas Merton, *The Seven Storey Mountain* , pp. 264–265. © Harcourt, Brace & Company. All rights reserved.

Small Group
HANDOUT

WEEK 7: PENTECOST 22
A Call to Christian Citizenship
Matthew 22:15–22

 **GATHERING**
10 min.

 **STUDY**
30 min.

 **CARING**
20–40 min.

Leader: The agenda has three parts. In the Gathering time you'll be getting to know each other through an "ice-breaker." This will be for your total group. The Study time has two parts: (1) Story and (2) Scripture. If you are short of time, skip the Story and move to the Scripture. Begin by reading out loud the Story or the Scripture to the whole group. Then divide into groups of 4 for the Study time. Finally, regather the total group for the Caring time. Keep to this agenda: (1) Gathering—10 minutes, (2) Study—30 minutes, and (3) Caring—20–40 minutes.

 **Final Round of Jeopardy.** As most people who have watched the TV game show *Jeopardy* know, the final round involves having the players decide how much of what they have won they are going to risk wagering on one final category. The category is given and players decide how much they will risk, depending on what the subject is, and how far behind or ahead they are. Imagine you are playing the game and you are behind $5,000 to $4,000. How much of your $4,000 are you going to risk if the final category is the following:

_____ understanding the opposite sex	_____ current rock groups
_____ Federal Income Tax forms	_____ auto mechanics
_____ names in the Old Testament	_____ soap opera couples
_____ politically correct language	_____ popular video games

<table>
<tr><td>SESSION

7</td><td><h1>A Call to Christian Citizenship</h1>
Pentecost 22 - Matthew 22:15–22</td></tr>
</table>

PURPOSE

To understand how God calls us to subject our allegiance to our country to our greater allegiance to God.

FOR THE PASTOR

The following material you can use as input for your sermon preparation on this week's Gospel Scripture from the book of Matthew. For further input you may want to share and further comment on the story of the ten Boom family, which your study group(s) will be responding to during their session. Also, it's important to share in your sermon or homily your own response to the personal question (or other personally-oriented question) to model personal sharing for your congregation.

SCRIPTURE

[15]Then the Pharisees went and plotted to entrap him in what he said. [16]So they sent their disciples to him, along with the Herodians, saying, "Teacher, we know that you are sincere, and teach the way of God in accordance with truth, and show deference to no one; for you do not regard people with partiality. [17]Tell us, then, what you think. Is it lawful to pay taxes to the emperor, or not?" [18]But Jesus, aware of their malice, said, "Why are you putting me to the test, you hypocrites? [19]Show me the coin used for the tax." And they brought him a denarius. [20]Then he said to them, "Whose head is this, and whose title?" [21]They answered, "The emperor's." Then he said to them, "Give therefore to the emperor the things that are the emperor's, and to God the things that are God's." [22]When they heard this, they were amazed; and they left him and went away.

Matthew 22:15–22

INTRODUCTION

We live in a country where groups like the "Freemen" of Montana have sought to declare that they are not subject to the United States government. Their actions gained a lot of national attention, which is perhaps what they wanted. But the issue they raised is not unlike an issue that has faced the church since the beginning of its existence—what loyalty and allegiance do we owe to the national government under which we live? The early church was often accused of being against civil government, and as a result they became more subject to persecution by Rome. This prompted Paul to make some strong statements urging Christians to citizenship and allegiance to their government (see Rom.

13:1–7). Still, Paul and Peter did defy their government on occasion in preaching the Gospel when ordered not to (see Acts 4:13–20). The bottom line seems to be that while members of Christ's Church are called to citizenship, they are called to Christian citizenship, which means keeping that allegiance subject to their greater allegiance to God. Responding to God's call means maintaining that perspective.

NOTES ON THE TEXT

22:15 *Pharisees.* These were members of a powerful religious sect whose prime concern was knowing and keeping the Law in all its detail.

22:16 *Herodians.* This was a political group made up of influential Jewish sympathizers of King Herod. Normally despised by the Pharisees as traitors who worked with Rome and associated with the Gentiles, the Pharisees would need this group's assistance to secure the civil authority's opposition to Jesus.

22:17 *taxes.* An annual poll tax had to be paid to the Romans by all adult Jews. Many Jews felt that paying taxes to the emperor (Caesar) was a denial of the belief that God was the rightful ruler of Israel. At least one anti-tax rebellion had already been crushed.

22:18 *aware of their malice.* Jesus knew they were trying to trap him. If he spoke against taxes, they would have grounds to charge him before the Roman authorities. If he spoke for them, he would lose much of his following.

22:19 *coin.* Only the denarius, a small silver coin, could be used to pay the poll tax. Since it bore the picture of Tiberius Caesar and a description of him as "Son of the Divine Augustine"—(i.e. a man touched with divinity), these coins were especially offensive to strict Jews who would not even handle them.

22:21 Jesus defused the intense emotional issue of taxes by minimizing its significance (i.e. "If the coin has Caesar's picture on it, then give it to him") while referring also to the importance of fidelity to God whose image is indelibly stamped upon all of humanity (Genesis 1:26).

PERSONAL QUESTION

The Pharisees sought to flatter Jesus as a set-up. If someone sought to flatter you, what should they focus on to have the best shot?

The ten Boom Family Confronts Nationalism. Corrie ten Boom's family sheltered Jews from the Nazis in Holland during World War II. But even before the war came, they learned directly of what German Nationalism was through the person of a young German supporter of Hitler who came to Holland to learn the watch repair trade. In their experience with this young German we see something of what happens when patriotism is made into a god. Their experience is told in this segment from *The Hiding Place:*

"Only once did the changes taking place in Germany reach inside the little shop on the Barteljorisstraat, and that was in the person of a young German watchmaker. Germans frequently came to work under father for a while, for his reputation reached even beyond Holland. So when this tall good-looking young man appeared with apprentice papers from a good firm in Berlin, Father hired him without hesitation. ...

"His first morning at work he came upstairs for coffee and Bible reading with the other employees; after that he sat alone down in the shop. When we asked him why, he said that though he had not understood the Dutch words, he had seen that Father was reading from the Old Testament which, he informed us, was the Jews' 'Book of Lies.'

"I was shocked, but Father was only sorrowful. 'He has been taught wrong,' he told me. 'By watching us, seeing that we love this Book and are truthful people, he will realize his error.'

"... In the end, Father did fire Otto—the first employee he had ever discharged in more than sixty years in business. And it was not the ... anti-Semitism that finally brought it about, but Otto's treatment of the old clock mender, Christoffels.

"From the very first I had been baffled by his brusqueness with the old man. ... One Sunday when Father, Betsie, and I were having dinner at Hilversum I commented on what I had concluded was simple thoughtlessness.

"Willem shook his head. 'It's very deliberate,' he said. 'It's because Christoffels is old. The old have no value to the State. They're also harder to train in the new ways of thinking. Germany is systematically teaching disrespect for old age.'

"We stared at him, trying to grasp such a concept. 'Surely, you are mistaken, Willem!' Father said. 'Otto is extremely courteous to me—unusually so. And I'm a good deal older than Christoffels.'

" 'You're different. You're the boss. That's another part of the system: respect for authority. It is the old and the weak who are to be eliminated.' [Corrie goes on to detail various acts of cruelty by Otto toward Christoffels.]

"... Father tried to reason with Otto as he let him go, to show him why such behavior was wrong. Otto did not answer. In silence he collected the few tools he had brought with him and in silence left the shop. It was only at the door that he turned to look at us, a look of the most utter contempt I had ever seen."[1]

[1]Corrie ten Boom, *The Hiding Place* (Minneapolis, MN: World Wide Publications, 1971), pp. 76–78.

Small Group
HANDOUT

WEEK 8: PENTECOST 23
A Call to Love
Matthew 22:34–46

 **GATHERING**
10 min.

 **STUDY**
30 min.

 **CARING**
20–40 min.

Leader: The agenda has three parts. In the Gathering time you'll be getting to know each other through an "ice-breaker." This will be for your total group. The Study time has two parts: (1) Story and (2) Scripture. If you are short of time, skip the Story and move to the Scripture. Begin by reading out loud the Story or the Scripture to the whole group. Then divide into groups of 4 for the Study time. Finally, regather the total group for the Caring time. Keep to this agenda: (1) Gathering—10 minutes, (2) Study—30 minutes, and (3) Caring—20–40 minutes.

 **Bulliish On People.** Over the past few weeks, we have "invested" in each other as a group. What kinds of investments have various group members turned out to be? Look at the list below and find a person in this group who best fits each category. Share these with each other in a spirit of affirmation.

BLUE-CHIP STOCK: the reliable one, performing steady and true

GROWTH STOCK: the one who has grown and "shot up" the most during these sessions

PASSBOOK SAVINGS: the one always available to the group

PRECIOUS METALS: the one showing their inherent (self) worth

COMMODITY FUTURES: the one showing a lot of potential for growth beyond this group

MUTUAL FUND: the one with diverse strengths that helped the group

REAL ESTATE: the one we invested a lot in, but got a lot in return

RARE ART: the one whose beauty as a person made them a pleasure to invest in

PURPOSE

To better see how responding to God's call means learning how to love others with the love of God.

FOR THE PASTOR

The following material you can use as input for your sermon preparation on this week's Gospel Scripture from the book of Matthew. For further input you may want to share and further comment on the story of the ten Boom family, which your study group(s) will be responding to during their session. Also, it's important to share in your sermon or homily your own response to the personal question (or other personally-oriented question) to model personal sharing for your congregation.

SCRIPTURE

[34] When the Pharisees heard that he had silenced the Sadducees, they gathered together, [35] and one of them, a lawyer, asked him a question to test him. [36] "Teacher, which commandment in the law is the greatest?" [37] He said to him, " 'You shall love the Lord your God with all your heart, and with all your soul, and with all your mind.' [38] This is the greatest and first commandment. [39] And a second is like it: 'You shall love your neighbor as yourself.' [40] On these two commandments hang all the law and the prophets."

[41] Now while the Pharisees were gathered together, Jesus asked them this question: [42] "What do you think of the Messiah? Whose son is he?" They said to him, "The Son of David." [43] He said to them, "How is it then that David by the Spirit calls him Lord, saying,

[44] 'The Lord said to my Lord,

"Sit at my right hand,

until I put your enemies under your feet" '?

[45] If David thus calls him Lord, how can he be his son?" [46] No one was able to give him an answer, nor from that day did anyone dare to ask him any more questions.

Matthew 22:34–46

INTRODUCTION

Above all, responding to God's call means responding to his call to love. If Jesus revealed anything about God, it was that God is love, and if God is love, then we must love those around us in obedient response to his love. This is not easy, of course. We are called to love people who may be irritating to us. We are called to love people whose culture makes their ways sometimes totally incomprehensible. But perhaps hardest of all, we are called to love the people we live with, whose foibles we must contend with daily. It's like what one child wrote in *Children's Letters to God:* "Dear God, I bet it is hard for you to love all of everybody in the whole world. There are only four people in our family and I can never do it."[1] Though loving as God calls us to do is hard, that does not diminish the fact we are called to do it. The good news, of course, is that we have a loving, powerful God to strengthen us for the challenge.

22:36 *which commandment ... is the greatest?* Some religious authorities sought to reduce all law to a few foundational principles. The Pharisees, who generally regarded all of the law as equally important, probably hoped Jesus would isolate one law and thus provide them with the opportunity to discredit him for ignoring other laws.

22:37 This is part of the Shema (Deut. 6:4–5). This passage, recited by pious Jews each morning and evening, captures what was essential about people's relationship to God. ***love.*** In Greek, this is Agape, an active, benevolent giving to others. Agape is rooted in the experience of God's unconditional love which frees up a person to love others without expectation of reward. ***heart / soul / mind.*** Mark's version is slightly different but amounts to the same thing: the point is to love God with one's entire being.

22:39 By adding this quote from Leviticus 19:18, Jesus may have been the first to directly connect loving God with loving people (although this equation is found in Jewish literature written around the same time as the Gospels; see also Luke 10:27 where the scribe makes this connection).

22:40 *the law and the prophets.* This is a shorthand way of referring to the entire Old Testament as it is found today. ***hang.*** As a door is supported and controlled by its hinges, so these commands support and control all interpretation and application of the religious law.

22:41–46 There was a debate going on at this time about the Messiah. Some said he would be a son of Levi; others (including the Pharisees) argued that the Messiah would come from the line of David. Jesus is not challenging the idea of Davidic sonship. He is, however, trying to get them to expand their view of who the Messiah is. If David acknowledges the Messiah's lordship this means that the Messiah must be something more than simply his descendant. He would not just be David's son, but God's son in a unique way.

How do you feel about bringing strangers into your home, as the ten Booms did?

The ten Booms Show God's Love to Jews. Corrie ten Boom and her family helped shelter Jews from the Nazis in the Holland of World War II, and for that faithfulness they were eventually sent to concentration camps. In the following segment from *The Hiding Place,* the ten Booms used code phrases to refer to people in need of hiding, like one Jew who had to make some adjustments of his own:

"... Even from the side of his head I could tell that this was our old-fashioned watch [code for a Jew with stereotypical features]. His form, his clothes, his very stance were music-hall-comedy Jewish.

"I ran down to the door. 'Do come in.'

"The smiling slender man in his early thirties, with his protruding ears, balding head, and miniscule glasses, gave an elaborate bow. I liked him instantly. ...

"Meyer Mossel, he told us afterward, had been a cantor in the synagogue in Amsterdam. For all his lightheartedness he had suffered much. Most of his family had been arrested; his wife and children were in hiding on a farm in the north which had declined to accept Meyer—'for obvious reasons,' he said with a grimace at his own unmistakable features. ...

"Changing Meyer's name was easy—at once he became 'Eusie.' But getting Eusie to eat non-kosher food was something else. The problem of course was that we were grateful for food of any kind: we stood in line for hours, this third year of the occupation, to get whatever was available.

"One day the paper announced that coupon number four was good for pork sausage. It was the first meat we'd had in weeks. ...

" 'Eusie,' Betsie said as she carried the steaming casserole of pork and potatoes to the table, 'the day has come.' ...

"Betsie placed a helping of sausage and potato before him. 'Bon appetit.'

"The tantalizing odor reached our meat-starved palates. Eusie wet his lips with his tongue. 'Of course,' he said, 'there's a provision for this in the Talmud.' He speared the meat with his fork, bit hungrily and rolled his eyes heavenward in pure pleasure. 'And I'm going to start hunting for it, too,' he said, 'just as soon as dinner's over' "[2]

[1]Compiled by Stuart Hample and Eric Marshall, *Children's Letters to God* (New York: Workman Publishing, 1991).
[2]Corrie ten Boom, *The Hiding Place* (Minneapolis, MN: World Wide Publications, 1971), pp. 114–116.

Small Group
HANDOUT

WEEK 9: PENTECOST 24
A Call to Humility
Matthew 23:1–12

 **GATHERING**
10 min.

 **STUDY**
30 min.

 **CARING**
20–40 min.

Leader: The agenda has three parts. In the Gathering time you'll be getting to know each other through an "ice-breaker." This will be for your total group. The Study time has two parts: (1) Story and (2) Scripture. If you are short of time, skip the Story and move to the Scripture. Begin by reading out loud the Story or the Scripture to the whole group. Then divide into groups of 4 for the Study time. Finally, regather the total group for the Caring time. Keep to this agenda: (1) Gathering—10 minutes, (2) Study—30 minutes, and (3) Caring—20–40 minutes.

 **Vacation Week.** Use the questions below to get acquainted. Go around the group on the first question. Then go around on the next question.

1. If you were to describe your past week as a vacation, would it be more like ...
- ❐ a Caribbean cruise—smooth sailing all the way
- ❐ a backpacking trip—carrying some burdens, but experiencing some great things
- ❐ a safari—a lot of frightening stuff, but still an adventure
- ❐ a day at the beach—until I got hit by the tidal wave
- ❐ a car trip across the back roads of America—I keep getting lost, but I've got all the time in the world.
- ❐ a canoe trip with my canoe overturned—I've lost everything, so how can I go on?

2. If you were writing home from this trip to convince everyone you were having a good time, what event would you point to as the highlight of your trip?

A Call to Humility
Pentecost 24 - Matthew 23:1–12

PURPOSE

To explore what it means that we are called to humility in Jesus Christ.

FOR THE PASTOR

The following material you can use as input for your sermon preparation on this week's Gospel Scripture from the book of Matthew. For further input you may want to share and further comment on the story of Desmond Tutu, which your study group(s) will be responding to during their session. Also, it's important to share in your sermon or homily your own response to the personal question (or other personally-oriented question) to model personal sharing for your congregation.

SCRIPTURE

23 *Then Jesus said to the crowds and to his disciples, 2"The scribes and the Pharisees sit on Moses' seat; 3therefore, do whatever they teach you and follow it; but do not do as they do, for they do not practice what they teach. 4They tie up heavy burdens, hard to bear, and lay them on the shoulders of others; but they themselves are unwilling to lift a finger to move them. 5They do all their deeds to be seen by others; for they make their phylacteries broad and their fringes long. 6They love to have the place of honor at banquets and the best seats in the synagogues, 7and to be greeted with respect in the marketplaces, and to have people call them rabbi. 8But you are not to be called rabbi, for you have one teacher, and you are all students. 9And call no one your father on earth, for you have one Father—the one in heaven. 10Nor are you to be called instructors, for you have one instructor, the Messiah. 11The greatest among you will be your servant. 12All who exalt themselves will be humbled, and all who humble themselves will be exalted.*

Matthew 23:1–12

INTRODUCTION

During the era of the "Me Generation" the word "humility" was determined to be a word for previous generations only. The new generation was going to stop denying self for the sake of children and society, and was instead going to seek "self-fulfillment." But the result of that ethic was a high divorce rate, and a generation of disturbed and violent children. Now we need to take a new look at what humility might mean, and what it means to put our own needs on the back burner in order to focus on others. Sure, some in the past have been humble and subservient to a fault, totally losing their sense of self-worth and their identity. But the opposite extreme is equally fallacious, as people forget what it means to live for something beyond self, resulting in a breakdown of society. Letting Christ direct us, as the one who valued himself and fulfilled his tremendous potential, and yet also gave himself for the world, will help us also find the balance.

23:2 *Moses' seat.* This refers to the seat in the front of each synagogue in which a rabbi sat while teaching.

23:4 *tie up heavy burdens.* Originally, the Pharisees were concerned with defining the meaning of the Law so that its intent could be applied to everyday life. However, over time this developed into such a complex, rigid tradition that it was nearly impossible for any working person to have time to observe it. As a result, the majority of people were trapped in an unending feeling of guilt. Rather than helping the people obey the Law and draw near to God, the tradition only alienated people all the more.

23:5 *phylacteries.* These were small cases made of parchment or leather containing a piece of vellum on which were inscribed texts of the Law. They were tied to the forehead and left arm. ***fringes.*** These were attached to their robes to remind them of God's commands. Apparently the Pharisees wore these in an ornamental way to draw attention to themselves.

23:6 *best seats in the synagogues.* The choice seat was up front, with its back to the box which contained the sacred Scriptures and its front facing the congregation so all would see who sat there.

23:7 *greeted.* Out of respect for the authority of the teachers of the law, people rose and called out titles of respect when they passed by. ***rabbi.*** This official title for the scribes literally meant "my master."

23:8–10 These verses, unique to Matthew, may have meant to prevent the rise of a sort of "Christian rabbinism" within this church community of Jewish converts.

23:11–12 This principle is a common theme in the Gospels (Matt. 18:4; Mark 9:35; Luke 14:11).

Who do you know who best exemplifies your definition of what it means to be "humble"?

Desmond Tutu Chooses Soweto. Desmond Tutu has become known around the world because of leading his people in the fight against apartheid in South Africa. An important step in that fight was when he was appointed as Dean of Johannesburg, the first time in history that a black man was to occupy office in that large, wealthy and vibrant diocese. His biographer, Shirley Duboulay tells of his struggle with one of the "perks" of that office in *Tutu: Voice of the Voiceless:*

"The arrival of a black Dean was front-page news in many of the South African papers, itself a comment on the crazy society apartheid creates. One of the consequences of his appointment that drew considerable attention was the question of where the Tutus should live. As all the previous Deans had been white, the deanery was in a white suburb, the affluent area of Houghton. Despite the Group Areas Act, in which residential areas are determined by race, the Tutus were invited to move into the official residence, but they adamantly refused to become 'honorary whites,' electing instead to share the conditions of their fellow blacks by living in Soweto. After owning his own house in a pleasant leafy suburb of London, Tutu was even more conscious than most black people of the poverty, dreariness and inadequacy of the conditions under which they were expected to live. ...

"It should be added that black South Africans are daily reminded of how they could live—if they were white. Daily they see the cars speed along fast, wide motorways, taking their owners the short distance to rich residential areas with smart houses, usually with their own swimming pools; they know that there the air is clear, the streets lit and the gardens bright with flowers. Daily, as they enter Soweto, which in 1975 still had no electricity, they pass the huge generator which feeds only the white areas; they return to unmade-up roads, dark streets, small back yards and the murky atmosphere which rises from several thousand coal stoves. There is a swimming pool—one, built at Father Huddlestone's initiative and shared by 1 million people.

"... If some people were disappointed that Tutu missed an opportunity to crack the Group Areas Act by living in Houghton, many more were delighted at this symbolic gesture of identification with his people."[1]

---

[1] Shirley DuBoulay, *Tutu: Voice of the Voiceless* (London, England: Hodder & Stoughton Publishers, 1988), pp. 96-97.

Small Group
HANDOUT

WEEK 10: PENTECOST 25
A Call to Readiness
Matthew 25:1–13

 **GATHERING**
10 min.

 **STUDY**
30 min.

 **CARING**
20–40 min.

Leader: The agenda has three parts. In the Gathering time you'll be getting to know each other through an "ice-breaker." This will be for your total group. The Study time has two parts: (1) Story and (2) Scripture. If you are short of time, skip the Story and move to the Scripture. Begin by reading out loud the Story or the Scripture to the whole group. Then divide into groups of 4 for the Study time. Finally, regather the total group for the Caring time. Keep to this agenda: (1) Gathering—10 minutes, (2) Study—30 minutes, and (3) Caring—20–40 minutes.

 **My Life's an Open Book.** If your life were a book, which of the following books would it be?

THE LITTLE ENGINE THAT COULD—I could have given up!

GREAT EXPECTATIONS—I could never live up to them!

GREEN EGGS AND HAM—I live in fear of what's in my refrigerator!

THE CALL OF THE WILD—I'm an outdoors person.

SENSE AND SENSIBILITY—I try to live life logically.

THE DEERSLAYER—I love to hunt!

LITTLE HOUSE ON THE PRAIRIE—I'm focused on home and family.

PILGRIM'S PROGRESS—My journey has been through many obstacles.

A Call to Readiness
Pentecost 25 - Matthew 25:1–13

PURPOSE

To understand how responding to God's call means being ready for what God might bring into our future, even if that might be the end of time.

FOR THE PASTOR

The following material you can use as input for your sermon preparation on this week's Gospel Scripture from the book of Matthew. For further input you may want to share and further comment on the story of Corrie ten Boom, which your study group(s) will be responding to during their session. Also, it's important to share in your sermon or homily your own response to the personal question (or other personally-oriented question) to model personal sharing for your congregation.

SCRIPTURE

25 *"Then the kingdom of heaven will be like this. Ten bridesmaids took their lamps and went to meet the bridegroom. ²Five of them were foolish, and five were wise. ³When the foolish took their lamps, they took no oil with them; ⁴but the wise took flasks of oil with their lamps. ⁵As the bridegroom was delayed, all of them became drowsy and slept. ⁶But at midnight there was a shout, 'Look! Here is the bridegroom! Come out to meet him.' ⁷Then all those bridesmaids got up and trimmed their lamps. ⁸The foolish said to the wise, 'Give us some of your oil, for our lamps are going out.' ⁹But the wise replied, 'No! there will not be enough for you and for us; you had better go to the dealers and buy some for yourselves.' ¹⁰And while they went to buy it, the bridegroom came, and those who were ready went with him into the wedding banquet; and the door was shut. ¹¹Later the other bridesmaids came also, saying, 'Lord, lord, open to us.' ¹²But he replied, 'Truly I tell you, I do not know you.' ¹³Keep awake therefore, for you know neither the day nor the hour."*

Matthew 25:1–13

INTRODUCTION

"Ready or not, here I come!" That's what children say in "hide-and -seek" when the "seeker" is through counting, and is ready to go look for the other children. Well, in many respects that's what God says to us. God will act in our world. God will act to redeem that world, and God will act to judge the world. The redemption of the world is his top priority, and God wants us to be part of that redemption; but if we refuse to be part of that redemption, or if we simply procrastinate so as to miss out on our chance to be part of the redemption, we will be making ourselves liable to his judgment! Whether we are ready or not, God is coming. Will his coming mean redemption or judgment for us? The choice is ours. We make that choice when we decide whether or not to live in obedience to Christ as Lord, so that we can be found doing his will when he comes.

25:1 *took their lamps.* Weddings typically occurred at night. The lamps, small earthen jars with a wick inserted to draw the oil used as fuel, would be held up on poles to brighten the way for the procession. *to meet the bridegroom.* Prior to a wedding, the groom would go to the bride's home and lead her in a procession to his house where the wedding would take place. These ten women were probably either at the bride's house or somewhere along the processional route waiting for the groom to come. Attending such a wedding was a great privilege, and these maidens would be eager to be part of it. The parable follows the lead of the Old Testament in picturing God (or, in this context, the Messiah) as the groom comes to take Israel as his bride (Isaiah. 54:4–5; 62:4; Ezekiel. 16:7; Hosea 2:19). The maidens are those who are to attend to God's people while they await the coming of the Lord.

25:3 *took no oil with them.* The only fuel for their lamps was whatever was left in the earthen lamps from the last use.

25:5 *the bridegroom was delayed.* The early Christians thought Christ would come again within their lifetime. As time went on this, of course, did not occur. Matthew, as well as other early Christians, would have identified Christ with this delayed bridegroom.

25:6 *at midnight.* This emphasizes the unexpected delay of the groom since this would have been long after most people would have expected him to come. *Come out to meet him.* People would gather around the groom to escort him to the bride's home and then back to the actual site of the wedding. The unexpected arrival of the groom, the shout of proclamation, and the people coming out to meet him all echo themes of the return of Christ as described in 1 Thessalonians 4:16–17.

25:8 *our lamps are going out.* Once the time for the procession arrived, the foolish women realized they were short on oil. This lack of preparation corresponds to those who await Christ's return, but without the preparation of doing the good deeds that give light to the world (Matt. 5:16).

25:9 *go to the dealers and buy.* Since it was so late, it would have been very difficult to find a shopkeeper open and willing to sell oil. At the time of the Lord's return, it is too late to make up for one's lack of preparation.

25:13 *Keep awake.* This is the essential point of the parable. We must keep awake to Christ's coming, and remain prepared by what we are doing in Christ's name.

What was the closest you have come to having to prepare for a "test" like Corrie ten Boom went through?

Corrie ten Boom Readies for a "Visit." Corrie ten Boom and her family sheltered Jews from the Nazis during World War II. This was of course dangerous work. They sought to make some practical preparations for the possibility that the Nazis might hear of their operation and make an unexpected raid. They put in a warning buzzer and had drills with their Jewish tenants, seeing how quickly they could be ushered into a secret room in the house; and prepared for possible questioning. Corrie writes of this in her book, *The Hiding Place*:

"That was the hardest. Never knowing. And one of the biggest unknowns was my own performance under questioning. As long as I was awake I felt fairly sure of myself. But if they should come at night. ... Over and over again the group worked with me—Nils, Henk, Leendert—bursting into my room without warning, shaking me awake, hurling questions at me.

"The first time it happened I was sure the real raid had come. There was a terrific pounding on my door, then the beam of a flashlight in my eyes. 'Get up! On your feet!' I could not see the man who was speaking.

" 'Where are you hiding your nine Jews?'

" 'We only have six Jews now.'

"There was an awful silence. The room light came on to show Rolf clutching his head with his hands. 'Oh no. Oh no,' he kept saying. 'It can't be that bad.'

" 'Think now,' said Henk just behind him. 'The Gestapo is trying to trap you. The answer is, "What Jews! We don't have Jews here." '

" 'Can I try again?'

" 'Not now,' said Rolf. 'You're wide-awake now.'

"They tried again a few nights later. 'The Jews you're hiding, where do they come from?'

"I sat up groggily. 'I don't know. They just come to the door.'

"Rolf flung his hat to the floor. 'No, no, no!' he shouted. "What Jews! There are no Jews!" Can't you learn?'

" 'I'll learn,' I promised. 'I'll do better.'

"And sure enough the next time I woke a little more completely. Half a dozen shadowy forms filled the room. 'Where do you hide the ration cards?' a voice demanded.

"Under the bottom stair, of course. But this time I would not be trapped into saying so. A crafty reply occurred to me: 'In the Frisian clock on the stairwell!'

"Kik sat down beside me on the bed and put an arm around me. 'That was better, Tante Corrie,' he said. 'You tried, this time. But remember—you have no cards except for you, Opa and Tante Betsie. There is no underground activity here, you don't understand what they're talking about. ...'

"Gradually, with repeated drills, I got better. Still, when the time actually came, when they were real Gestapo agents really trained in getting the truth from people, how would I perform?"[1]

---

[1] Corrie ten Boom, *The Hiding Place* (Minneapolis, MN: World Wide Publications, 1971), pp.126–127.

Small Group

HANDOUT

WEEK 11: PENTECOST 26

A Call to Risk

Matthew 25:14–30

 **GATHERING**
10 min.

 **STUDY**
30 min.

 **CARING**
20–40 min.

Leader: The agenda has three parts. In the Gathering time you'll be getting to know each other through an "ice-breaker." This will be for your total group. The Study time has two parts: (1) Story and (2) Scripture. If you are short of time, skip the Story and move to the Scripture. Begin by reading out loud the Story or the Scripture to the whole group. Then divide into groups of 4 for the Study time. Finally, regather the total group for the Caring time. Keep to this agenda: (1) Gathering—10 minutes, (2) Study—30 minutes, and (3) Caring—20–40 minutes.

 **A Winning Team.** Imagine that your small group has been a basketball team, playing the season together. A winning team requires that people be willing to play different roles. What roles have you seen people playing in the group? Put the name of a different person from your group next to each of the following roles. Then have people share what roles they saw each other playing:

__________POINT GUARD—the one who got everyone else involved

__________SLAM DUNKER—the one who really "drove home" some good points

__________LONG-RANGE SHOOTER—the one who helped us think ahead

__________DEFENSIVE SPECIALIST—the one who kept things from getting out of hand

__________INSPIRATIONAL LEADER—the combination player and cheerleader who lifted us up when we needed it

__________QUIET CONTRIBUTOR—the one who helped the team in so many ways without getting much attention for it

__________POWER FORWARD—the one who was willing to "get tough" when we had to face tough issues

<table>
<tr><td>SESSION
11</td><td>

A Call to Risk
Pentecost 26 - Matthew 25:14–30

</td></tr>
</table>

PURPOSE

To see how responding to God's call means being willing to take risks when we believe God is calling us to do so.

FOR THE PASTOR

The following material you can use as input for your sermon preparation on this week's Gospel Scripture from the book of Matthew. For further input you may want to share and further comment on the story of Billy Graham, which your study group(s) will be responding to during their session. Also, it's important to share in your sermon or homily your own response to the personal question (or other personally-oriented question) to model personal sharing for your congregation.

SCRIPTURE

[14]"For it is as if a man, going on a journey, summoned his slaves and entrusted his property to them; [15]to one he gave five talents, to another two, to another one, to each according to his ability. Then he went away. [16]The one who had received the five talents went off at once and traded with them, and made five more talents. [17]In the same way, the one who had the two talents made two more talents. [18]But the one who had received the one talent went off and dug a hole in the ground and hid his master's money. [19]After a long time the master of those slaves came and settled accounts with them. [20]Then the one who had received the five talents came forward, bringing five more talents, saying, 'Master, you handed over to me five talents; see, I have made five more talents.' [21]His master said to him, 'Well done, good and trustworthy slave; you have been trustworthy in a few things, I will put you in charge of many things; enter into the joy of your master.' [22]And the one with the two talents also came forward, saying, 'Master, you handed over to me two talents; see, I have made two more talents.' [23]His master said to him, 'Well done, good and trustworthy slave; you have been trustworthy in a few things, I will put you in charge of many things; enter into the joy of your master.' [24]Then the one who had received the one talent also came forward, saying, 'Master, I knew that you were a harsh man, reaping where you did not sow, and gathering where you did not scatter seed; [25]so I was afraid, and I went and hid your talent in the ground. Here you have what is yours.' [26]But his master replied, 'You wicked and lazy slave! You knew, did you, that I reap where I did not sow, and gather where I did not scatter? [27]Then you ought to have invested my money with the bankers, and on my return I would have received what was my own with interest. [28]So take the talent from him, and give it to the one with the ten talents. [29]For to all those who have, more will be given, and they will have an abundance; but from those who have nothing, even what they have

will be taken away. ³⁰As for this worthless slave, throw him into the outer darkness, where there will be weeping and gnashing of teeth.'

Matthew 25:14–30

INTRODUCTION

Ever since grade school most of us have become familiar with "talent shows." These were generally opportunities for people with the performance talents of singing, acting or playing musical instruments to showcase their abilities. Such shows can be a lot of fun. But the bad part of this is that with such events many people get the idea that if they don't have such performance talents, they don't have talents. A person who plays the piano well is "talented." But what about a person who has the necessary skills to be an excellent friend in time of need? What about a person who can always diagnose, almost by instinct, what is wrong with a car? The truth is, all of life is a talent show. God has given us many kinds of talents, and each moment of life is an opportunity to showcase them. Of course, we aren't really called to use these talents to entertain others, and that is the difference. What we are called on to use them for is to please God and to serve him. But we can still applaud! We can applaud the God who has given us these talents, we can applaud the fact that all of us have them, and we can applaud each other as we use them to the glory of God.

NOTES ON
THE TEXT

25:14 *it is as if.* "It" refers to the kingdom of heaven (see Matthew 25:1). The kingdom starts here and now with responsible stewardship, which this parable is about. ***entrusted his property to them.*** Wealthy people who had to travel on business would entrust their resources to capable servants who would act as managers of the estate. Their responsibility was to look after their master's interests in his absence, investing his resources in a way that would earn more money for him.

25:15 *five talents.* "Talent" originally referred to a measure of weight. Later it became a monetary measure, equal to about $1,000 in silver or gold. In modern English our word "talent," which means an ability, derives from this parable.

25:18 *dug a hole.* This was a common way of hiding money, and is the way many ancient coins have been preserved and found by archaeologists.

25:26 *I reap where I did not sow.* While this is meant to be a parable of what God has entrusted to us, we must be careful not to try to make too exact a parallel between God and this miserly master. A parable was meant to have one central point, in this case that what God gives us he expects us to use responsibly. There was no intent to make all the comparisons exact. We should not then try to argue from this parable that God is harsh and greedy. Jesus gave his life to show just the' opposite— that God's love and grace is abundant!

25:27 *... with interest.* When interest was charged in ancient times, rates were high. However, in most cases Jews were discouraged from charging interest, especially to the poor. Romans and Greeks, however, had no such scruples.

25:30 *weeping and gnashing of teeth.* This is a typical phrase used to describe what happens in hell. The parable here has gone to describing not what happened to the servant in the parable, but what will happen to the one who does not use what God has given in service to God.

Billy Graham didn't feel he had a very adequate education. What personal shortcoming are you especially conscious of?

Billy Graham Wrestles With His Calling. Billy Graham is one of the best-known Christians of the 20th century. Many thousands of people have responded to his resonant voice as he has called them to make a commitment to Jesus Christ. But even so, responding to his own call to ministry was far from automatic for him. His biographer, John Pollock, writes of Billy's struggle in the book, *To All the Nations: The Billy Graham Story:*

"An even stronger influence began to shape him. Temple Terrace had become a vacation attraction to prominent evangelicals from North and South. ... He listened attentively as they discoursed on the decline of religion in America—church budgets low, church buildings emptying, church preaching blunted and confused. These old stalwarts who had seen the fires die down had one theme: we need a prophet. We need a man to call America back to God.

"A 'tremendous burden' began to weigh on Billy Graham. On walks at night across the golf course and along the open streets, laid out for housing estates never built, he faced his future. He believed he would not make a preacher: he was too poorly educated. Yet he began to sense an unmistakable call. Praying aloud as he walked the empty countryside he answered that call in Moses' words at the burning bush: 'They will not believe me, nor harken unto my voice ... . I am not eloquent.'

"... In the night walks alone he tussled with excuses. His indifferent background might indeed keep him a mediocre preacher 'somewhere out in the sticks.' Yet any sacrifice appeared trivial beside Christ's sufferings or the world's needs. As for eloquence, the Lord had told Moses, 'Go, and I will be with thy mouth, and teach thee what thou shalt say.' ...

"One night in March, 1938 Billy Graham returned from his walk and reached the eighteenth green ... . 'The trees were loaded with Spanish moss, and in the moonlight it was like a fairyland.' He sat down on the edge of the green, looking up at the moon and stars, aware of a warm breeze from the south. The tension snapped. 'I remember getting on my knees and saying, "O God, if you want me to preach, I will do it." ' "[1]

[1] John Pollock, *To All the Nations: The Billy Graham Story* (San Francisco: Harper & Row, 1985), pp. 21–22.

Small Group
HANDOUT

WEEK 12: LAST PENTECOST
A Call to Giving
Matthew 25:31–46

 **GATHERING**
10 min.

 **STUDY**
30 min.

 **CARING**
20–40 min.

Leader: The agenda has three parts. In the Gathering time you'll be getting to know each other through an "ice-breaker." This will be for your total group. The Study time has two parts: (1) Story and (2) Scripture. If you are short of time, skip the Story and move to the Scripture. Begin by reading out loud the Story or the Scripture to the whole group. Then divide into groups of 4 for the Study time. Finally, regather the total group for the Caring time. Keep to this agenda: (1) Gathering—10 minutes, (2) Study—30 minutes, and (3) Caring—20–40 minutes.

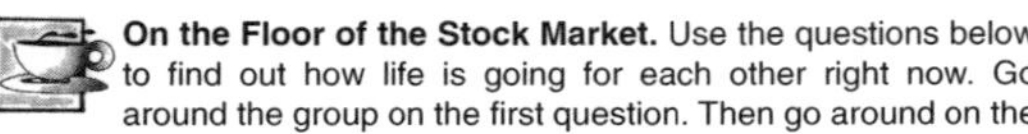 **On the Floor of the Stock Market.** Use the questions below to find out how life is going for each other right now. Go around the group on the first question. Then go around on the next question.

1. If your life this past week were the stock market, how would you describe this week's activity?
   - ❑ unchanged in active trading—a lot happening; some good, some bad
   - ❑ unchanged in light trading—nothing happened
   - ❑ closed slightly lower—no depression, but I may be going through a recession
   - ❑ closed slightly higher—Things are better, but nobody would get rich off of me.
   - ❑ a rally!—Everything I'm investing in is paying dividends!
   - ❑ a crash!—If I could have, I would have "suspended trading"!

2. If you were a broker, advising people whether to invest in you for the coming week, would you be more "bearish" (pessimistic) or more "bullish" (optimistic)?

<table>
<tr><td>SESSION
12</td><td><h1>A Call to Giving</h1>Last Pentecost - Matthew 25:31–46</td></tr>
</table>

PURPOSE

To come to an appreciation of the fact that a lifestyle of giving is central to what it means to respond to God's call.

FOR THE PASTOR

The following material you can use as input for your sermon preparation on this week's Gospel Scripture from the book of Matthew. For further input you may want to share and further comment on the story of Mother Teresa, which your study group(s) will be responding to during their session. Also, it's important to share in your sermon or homily your own response to the personal question (or other personally-oriented question) to model personal sharing for your congregation.

SCRIPTURE

[31] When the Son of Man comes in his glory, and all the angels with him, then he will sit on the throne of his glory. [32] All the nations will be gathered before him, and he will separate people one from another as a shepherd separates the sheep from the goats, [33] and he will put the sheep at his right hand and the goats at the left. [34] Then the king will say to those at his right hand, 'Come, you that are blessed by my Father, inherit the kingdom prepared for you from the foundation of the world; [35] for I was hungry and you gave me food, I was thirsty and you gave me something to drink, I was a stranger and you welcomed me, [36] I was naked and you gave me clothing, I was sick and you took care of me, I was in prison and you visited me.' [37] Then the righteous will answer him, 'Lord, when was it that we saw you hungry and gave you food, or thirsty and gave you something to drink? [38] And when was it that we saw you a stranger and welcomed you, or naked and gave you clothing? [39] And when was it that we saw you sick or in prison and visited you?' [40] And the king will answer them, 'Truly I tell you, just as you did it to one of the least of these who are members of my family, you did it to me.' [41] Then he will say to those at his left hand, "You that are accursed, depart from me into the eternal fire prepared for the devil and his angels; [42] for I was hungry and you gave me no food, I was thirsty and you gave me nothing to drink, [43] I was a stranger and you did not welcome me, naked and you did not give me clothing, sick and in prison and you did not visit me.' [44] Then they also will answer, 'Lord, when was it that we saw you hungry or thirsty or a stranger or naked or sick or in prison, and did not take care of you?' [45] Then he will answer them, 'Truly I tell you, just as you did not do it to one of the least of these, you did not do it to me.' [46] And these will go away into eternal punishment, but the righteous into eternal life."

Matthew 25:31–46

We are told that *all* Scripture is inspired by God, and most Christians believe that in some sense. But that does not negate the fact that *some* Scripture passages seem to speak to people and inspire them a little more than others. Of our Gospel passage for this week, renowned writer, teacher and evangelist Tony Campolo writes, "This passage of Scripture has become central to my preaching. There have been few sermons that I have preached over the past quarter of a century in which these verses have not been cited."[1] The centrality of this passage for Campolo is related to his own scripturally-inspired passion for the poor and oppressed people of our world. And when we look at this passage, which is one of the Bible's best story-pictures of what God expects of us, can any of us as followers of Christ be comfortable with ourself and our spiritual status if we don't have such a concern?

25:31 *Son of Man.* This is Jesus' favorite way of referring to himself, as opposed to the more popular (and more militaristic) Messianic title "Son of David." ***comes in his glory.*** Jesus came the first time "veiled in human form," but when he comes again his "glory," his divine nature, will be evident, as it was evident to those who witnessed the transfiguration (Matthew 17:1–8).

25:32 *All the nations.* Both those to be blessed and those to be cursed would include people of every nation, not just those of Israel. ***as a shepherd separates ...*** The sheep of Palestine are usually white and the goats black, so that a shepherd could easily separate them. These animals graced in common herds during the day. At night, however, they were separated because the goats needed to be in shelters to be protected from the elements.

25:33 *at his right hand.* The right hand was considered to be the side of honor and blessing.

25:34 *inherit the kingdom.* To inherit the kingdom meant to be recognized as a true child of God. The traditional Jewish doctrine of the day taught that one was a child of God just by virtue of being descended from Abraham. Hence all descendants of Abraham would be seen as inheriting the kingdom.

25:36 The actions commended are concrete acts of love to the most needy in society. ***in prison.*** Probably those (like John the Baptist) who were in prison because they resisted the state out of their fidelity to God are in view. It may also reflect the fact that many people were in prison because of their inability to pay off a debt. Hence, these too are the poor.

25:40 *who are members of my family ...* Does this phrase refer to all poor or to just those who are faithful? This is unclear and much debated. But in any case, Jesus here affirms that to love him one must minister to the poor.

PERSONAL QUESTION

When you were a child or adolescent, what "judge" did you most fear standing before: Your father or mother? A principal or teacher? An actual court judge?

STORY

Mother Teresa Sees Christ in the Poor. Mother Teresa has become well-known throughout the world for her work with "the poorest of the poor," especially in Calcutta, India. She insists, however, that this is more than just a kind of social work—it is God's work. Her biographer, Lush Gjergji, writes of this work and her philosophy behind it in the book, *Mother Teresa: Her Life, Her Works:*

"[Mother Teresa said] 'We are not social workers. We want to bring our people both happiness and divine love, God himself who loves them through us. Thus we love God by serving him through them. ...

"When visiting the poor, Mother Teresa came across many desperate situations. Every day she beheld people who were destined to die in the streets. From afar she could hear their lamentations. She stopped before them and her Voice said to her, 'Help them! At least let them die like human beings.' So she established at Calcutta the first refuge for the dying. This is the well-known *Nirmal Hriday* (Pure Heart) refuge, opened in 1954 at #14 Creek Lane.

"On one occasion she said: 'Our life is bound up with that of Jesus by means of holy communion. We receive Jesus under the appearance of bread; we must also recognize him in those around us, in others, in all people, in the poor and forsaken.

" 'Our meeting with Jesus in communion should prepare us to recognize and serve him in our neighbor, for Jesus himself said: "What you do to the least of my brothers, you do to me. I was rejected, and you took me in." '

"As Miguel Gomes relates, it all started like this:

" 'One day we found a dying man by the sidewalk, not far from Campbell Hospital, near our house. Mother Teresa went to the hospital to ask admission for this poor wretch. In vain. No room for him there. We went to a pharmacy to get some medicine, but when we returned he was already dead. Deeply moved, she said: "They take better care of their cats and dogs than of human beings." And with that she went to protest to the authorities.' "[2]

[1]Tony Campolo, *Can Mainline Denominations Make a Comeback?* (Valley Forge, PA, 1995), p. 20.
[2]Lush Gjergji, *Mother Teresa: Her Life, Her Works* (Hyde Park, NY: New City Press, 1991), pp. 56,58.